UPFRONT

UPFRONT
THE JEFF PROBYN STORY

JEFF PROBYN and BARRY NEWCOMBE

MAINSTREAM
PUBLISHING

EDINBURGH AND LONDON

For my family, and all the players in the England squad who are afraid to say what they think and all those out of it who can.

Jeff Probyn, Wasps and England.

First published in Great Britain in 1993 by
MAINSTREAM PUBLISHING COMPANY (EDINBURGH) LTD
7 Albany Street
Edinburgh EH1 3UG

ISBN 1 85158 554 0

A catalogue record for this book is available from the British Library

Typeset in Great Britain by Litho Link Limited, Welshpool, Powys
Printed in Great Britain by Butler & Tanner Ltd, Frome

CONTENTS

Acknowledgments   7

Chapter One   An Impossible Journey?   11
Chapter Two   My Nautical Connection   25
Chapter Three   The Call of Wasps   33
Chapter Four   Not Wanted on Voyage   45
Chapter Five   Australia Tamed   57
Chapter Six   Trying in Bucharest   65
Chapter Seven   The Alternative Tour   71
Chapter Eight   Grand Slump   77
Chapter Nine   All Things Argentine   85
Chapter Ten   The World Cup Story   93
Chapter Eleven   The Askean Connection   111
Chapter Twelve   Slam and Out   117
Chapter Thirteen   Geoff Cooke – My View   131
Chapter Fourteen   Will Carling – My View   139
Chapter Fifteen   The Money Game   145
Chapter Sixteen   Sole Alone   155
Chapter Seventeen My England Men   163
Chapter Eighteen   Left by the Lions   181

ACKNOWLEDGMENTS

Last December, at the annual dinner of the Sports Writers' Association in London, Jeff Probyn asked me if I would write this book for him. Flattered, and with a couple of glasses of Crozes Hermitage on board, I agreed – and the end product is in your hands.

We have talked many hours away in pursuit of the many factors which brought Jeff, a full-blooded, genuine Cockney, from the East End of London to the England rugby team and one of the great anchor positions of the world's greatest team game at tight-head prop.

I have known many England props over the last 30 years or so and Jeff Probyn maintains the dynasty. Ron Jacobs, once England's most capped prop, was my mentor when I first started to try to write about rugby as a cub reporter in Northampton in 1958. He was unfailingly kind and helpful to me, and if I know anything at all about what props try to do it goes back to what the farmer from the Fens with his massive hands and huge love of the game told me. Jacobs had a simple philosophy about the game – that forwards should win the ball and backs should not drop it.

Other characters followed in his wake. I think of the eternally durable Phil Judd and the voluble Keith Fairbrother from Coventry, of the angle-packing Tony Horton from Blackheath, of the mighty Fran Cotton, of Phil Blakeway and Robin Cowling who could and did play with injuries that would halt others, of Stack Stevens and Piggy Powell, men of the land. Cotton took Jacobs's record and Gary Pearce took his, and now Jeff Probyn is England's most capped prop with 37 caps, all of them achieved in his thirties. Mike Burton, another England man who knew his way around the front row, was trying to demonstrate to me late one night what Jeff does in scrums but gave up, saying: 'Let him tell you, he's his own man, as we all are.' Well, Jeff has told me what makes him the player he is and what has happened in his time in the England scrum alongside Brian Moore at hooker and firstly his old mate Paul Rendall and then Jason Leonard on the other side of the front row.

These words are virtually all from Jeff with my punctuation. He is a man who cares about his rugby and has an intensity of pride which is beyond normal measure. His feeling for wearing the England shirt goes much wider than you might imagine and he has never given one away without careful consideration of what he is doing.

All international prop forwards have emerged from a very individualistic physical training school to enter a game where contact with the opposition is assured. Jeff always believed he could meet those demands, and that is why he is today one of the legends of the England team, a double Grand Slam winner and World Cup finalist. Not bad for a man some said was too small or just plain illegal.

Being taken into the England front-row activities by one of its senior members has to be balanced against the fact that Jeff wants young props to be properly nurtured in the game and brought along with safety as a prerequisite. It would be a shame, in the fullness of time, if Jeff's experience is not utilised. Women are excepted – he thinks they have no place on the rugby field.

My thanks go to Mainstream for inspiring this book with Jeff in the first place, to the players who represent their sport with unchanging charm in a changing world, to my colleagues for their support, notably Terry Cooper, Chris Jones and Steve Jones, and to my daughter Kerry Newcombe who transferred each word on to the newest available technology. I would also like to thank the picture-desk staff of the *Sunday Express* and Colorsport for their assistance with photographs.

Barry Newcombe
Runfold, Surrey
July 1993

Chapter One

AN IMPOSSIBLE JOURNEY?

Some people might think it was an impossible journey, from the heart of London's East End, which is hardly known for its rugby pitches, all the way to the England team, to Twickenham and many other major grounds around the world – and all this from the age of 31 onwards. I am not saying for a moment that I saw a blinding flash of light and realised that I could play rugby for England. But from the time I first started realising what I could do on the pitch, probably in my late teens, I knew that I was good enough to make the top. I have always had that belief, and still have to this day. Without that belief you are on a lost cause. Ask anybody who has played international rugby and they will tell you that they always go on to the park believing they are better. I am sure the same argument applies to international sports people across the board.

I am a genuine East Ender, born there, raised there, working there. There would not be too many people in the cramped streets around my family furniture business in Shoreditch who would know that I am a rugby player, let alone an England rugby player. But that is where I come from, and if you think I am some kind of lone ranger from the East End who broke through into the England front row which is traditionally meant to be filled by men from the West Country or the Midlands and sometimes from the North I would ask you to think again. My fellow prop on the other side of the England front row when I first won selection in 1988 was Paul Rendall of Wasps. He was born in the London borough of Islington which is so close to the East End that he just about qualifies to be one of us. And when he left the England side in 1991, having won 28 caps, who should come in but yet another man who speaks my kind of language, Jason Leonard of Harlequins, born in Barking, Essex, just beyond the East End. I would say the three of us have created a modest dynasty for our part of the world.

Nobody could have warned me 20 years ago that I was going to become one of the players to share in rugby's revolution at the top. How could anyone have foreseen the staggering amount of change which has taken place and which is still continuing? It has been a revolution which has forced almost every international player in the world to rethink his attitude to the game, what he should put into it and what he can expect out of it now that the historical bonds of amateurism have been loosened, if not broken for ever. Every player in England has been touched to some degree by what has happened in club rugby because the revolution has filtered down from the top.

One obvious example is the England shirt which so many players aspire to wear. The shirt design, a red English rose on a plain white background, survived for more than 100 years until the new age of commercialism forced it out. I am one of the few England players who have worn the old shirt and its multi-coloured successors. But each England shirt I have pulled on has been a point of pride for me. I have never felt I was putting it on for just England and Jeff Probyn. I felt that I was taking that shirt on behalf of hundreds of props throughout the country who would have given so much to do what I was doing. I felt that responsibility because I know that selection for England is a matter of your number coming up, and there is never any guarantee of that from one match to the next. My feeling for the shirt may be different from others. I know of players who have wept when they have put it on for the first time. There are others for whom the shirt does not have much long-term meaning. But I know what has happened to all the England shirts I have worn, who I have swapped them with, and what sort of matches we had. I would never give an England shirt away lightly because it means so much to me.

I have worn a few other shirts along the way. I played for a variety of clubs around London before settling at Wasps in 1984. I broke away briefly from Wasps in 1991 and played in the World Cup that year as a member of the Kent club, Askeans, in what turned out to be a short-lived, one-match relationship. Wasps has basically been my home, and I have been to two Cup finals at Twickenham and won the League title with them. I have been part of Wasps as they have earned their place as one of the top two London clubs in England. In terms of the English player market there is room for only two London clubs in the First Division of the Courage Leagues and Wasps have proved their right to be one of them. The club has been caught up in the revolution as well. The clubhouse and spectator accommodation has changed considerably in a matter of years. The club has attracted high-quality sponsorship and hospitality packages, and other commercial activity – we even had a bookmaker set up on the ground at Sudbury – has become the name of the game.

Travelling around England with Wasps you can see mirror images in almost every big club. Harlequins, our only other rivals in London, are trying to put some character into their home at the Stoop ground which doubles as England's training headquarters prior to matches at Twickenham. Whenever I have been to Bath it has been to play before packed crowds for high stakes and no one can deny that on the pitch Bath have set standards for the rest of the clubs to follow. There was a time when Bath were providing the hard core of the England team and that could happen again because they continue to attract good players and have Jack Rowell as coach to help them still further. Look at what has happened to Ben Clarke in the last couple of years – he has gone from England prospect to being voted the man of the tour for the British Lions in New Zealand in 1993.

The clubs from the big cities and towns are basically dominating the League. There is a new realism around the game: you have to progress to survive and everyone is catching up as fast as they can. I look at Bristol and Gloucester who were the best clubs in the West Country when I began and can see that they are doing everything in their power to maintain their place and not be overshadowed by Bath. I have seen Leicester set high standards as a Cup-winning side over the years, and their huge crowds, the biggest in England, will be expecting success in the League as well. Northampton looked like fading out of the reckoning a few years ago, but with enlightened management and fresh playing policies have put themselves back into the picture in a major way.

Geographically, the power base of the First Division extends from Leicester to the south and west. As the 1993-94 season began the other clubs in the First Division were London Irish, who are going to be more dependent than ever on players coming across from Ireland, and the two northern clubs, Orrell in the west and Newcastle Gosforth in the east. With 18 matches, home and away, for the first time the League took players into a new era of commitment and demand. In this case the revolution was taking the game into the unknown. There are certain to be casualties in such intense competition and playing disciplines are under greater stress than ever before.

There have been other casualties from the League. When I began playing what was called first-class rugby, the top clubs included Coventry, Bedford and Moseley, Richmond, Blackheath and Rosslyn Park, London Welsh, London Scottish, and Saracens, Sale and Headingley. Some have faded altogether and may never regain the status which they enjoyed under the old-boy network of traditional fixture lists. Rugby has become much more cut-throat as the League has grown, but the expansion of matches at least prevents each game becoming like a Cup-tie.

The redevelopment of the English game has also broken up the rivalries with Welsh clubs which in my younger days were an absolutely fundamental part of the season. When I was playing with Richmond they had a long list of Welsh clubs opposing them and there were no easy games. When I moved to Wasps, the same applied and we had some tremendous games, home and away, against the Welsh boys. Up front, we had the sort of contests which props all over the world would relish. But the League has virtually killed off this rivalry even before the expansion of 1993–94. Friendly matches with Welsh clubs on non-League days became a real lottery because full teams were fielded only rarely and there was little at stake except pride. Players used to competing for League points found a certain lack of intensity. We were looking at the embers of the past rather than the fires of the present. As a prop I loved playing against any one of the top half dozen Welsh clubs. It was a method of measuring yourself because the Welsh boys know what it is all about and always seemed to have that little more to give against English opposition. Now I wonder if the relationship can ever come back. League rugby dominates Wales just as much as it does England from now on. There are just no gaps in the season and the English and Welsh games are growing apart.

I know people say an Anglo–Welsh league could bring the main clubs back together. But who is going to put that into place? Would the Rugby Union and the Welsh Rugby Union ever be mandated by their members to set up a joint league? Would it benefit so few that it would not be worth while? Might not an end of season eight-club play-off for an Anglo–Welsh title look more interesting and demand less time? Would the unions take a lead from a sponsor or television because any big show-down between England and Wales would have a high price tag? And when could it happen – the current League agreements still have some time to run in both countries?

Having experienced 'friendly' rugby and League rugby in my time I would question whether the intensity of the game is all that different. My memory is that we put plenty of thought and effort into matches long before League rugby arrived. The difference now lies in the depth of preparation which means that players come fitter and more highly motivated into League matches because so much could turn on a single result. Until this season, clubs could lose their first two matches and find themselves under threat of relegation from the outset. Maybe the expanded leagues will change that threat appearing as early as it did. I have not yet had to play under the pressure of avoiding a drop to the Second Division but I have seen plenty who have and you know when you have beaten them that it is a shattering experience.

I doubt whether the League has actually produced any more players of international quality than used to come through under the pre-League system. Genuine natural ability, of which someone like Jeremy Guscott is a rare example, surfaces all too infrequently. But it has been obvious to me that the English game is producing fitter players who can react better to pressure because pressure is what tests them in the League. Anyone holding a regular place in one of the top half dozen clubs in the First Division must know the business. This does not mean he can make the jump up to international football, but if he had to, under whatever circumstances, you could reasonably expect him not to let you down in the general run of play.

This is where the four divisions, London, Midlands, North and South-West, come into play. The Divisional Championship is another part of the revolution and I fully support it. Until you take a player out of the environment where he feels comfortable and understands virtually everything which is going on around him, and put him into a different environment where he feels less comfortable and more unpredictable, you cannot really know his value. There are plenty of examples of players using the Divisional Championship to state their cases. Will Carling was one. Ben Clarke was another. And there are many other examples.

I know that the Divisional Championship gets moved around from one year to the next to fit in with other commitments and I know that the crowds are not as large as perhaps they should be. But I regard the Championship as a proving ground, one step beyond club football, one step behind international football. It is also the framework for producing sides to play touring teams and in that sense London gave me my first foothold on my route to the England team when I came on as replacement against Andy Slack's Grand Slam Australians in 1984 at Twickenham. If the time and money can be found I would recommend stepping up divisional activity, and there is no lack of opposition around the world. The divisions ought to think in terms of playing French clubs, South African provinces, on a one-off basis, or making short tours of Australia or New Zealand. Closer to home, there are district teams in Scotland, Ireland, and Wales all suggesting themselves as opponents.

If we want the English game to sharpen itself for the future, contact with other nations is vital and the divisions can play their part in this. Regular exposure against Southern Hemisphere opposition should be a prerequisite of England planning at a variety of levels – and I totally agree with the New Zealand players who believe they should be playing England much more often than they do. It struck me as ludicrous that England and New Zealand played the first match of the World Cup in 1991, with all that meant to the competition, without having met anywhere since 1985. That is simply too big a gap and ways have to be found to close that. If tours come up too infrequently, why not arrange one-off matches?

People ask me why I did not win selection for England until I was 31, and the answer is the same whether you are in or whether you are out – it is up to a group of selectors. There is little you can do to influence things except play to the best of your ability. It has often been said that I was an illegal scrummager and that this frightened off selectors who considered that I would be penalised out of the game and that my team would suffer as a result. I have always disputed that supposition and contend that my style of scrummaging is perfectly legal. If I am called awkward, difficult, a nuisance, then I have to consider I am doing my job. No front-row forward who has the first point of contact with the opposition can be expected to be charitable. Everyone is looking for a weakness to exploit and although I am not saying that everything is evil in the front row, it is no place for the unwary.

I have been sent off a few times, but not recently, and suffered the usual crop of indignities that come your way in the front row. By that I mean eye-gouging, lip-tearing, biting, head-butting, stamping and punching. These things rarely happen all at once and the one thing age teaches you is to spot when they are coming and do something about it. Most of the cheap shots come from France and, to a lesser extent, Wales, but all of your opponents are capable of trying something and see how much they can get away with. Any team is prepared to go to different limits, providing they believe they will not get caught, and each team has a different way of doing this. The French are always up to something if you are causing them problems. They try to isolate you and work you over and you have to show them that you do not care and keep on doing your job. Wales went through a long period when they seemed to target people – Mike Teague, for example, was put off at Cardiff in 1989 – and we had to develop a system of blocking hit-men like Mark Jones so they could not inflict damage. Scotland play so much of their rugby off side that it has became an art form and Finlay Calder was the man who painted their masterpieces. Ireland have this organised-mayhem policy under which they used to blast at you for about an hour and then collapse, providing your own organisation and beliefs held good. But the Irish changed their act at Lansdowne Road in 1993 when they kept it going against England for an entire game. This was my 37th appearance for England, and Carling had asked me to lead the team out to mark the fact that this was a record for an England prop. Little did I realise when the England side followed me that we were about to suffer one of those humiliations that only Ireland can give you. Disrupt, divert, destroy, that was how the Irish saw it and we were not able to check them. But if you are going to lose, lose in Dublin, because it is the most hospitable place either way.

Regrettably, I have had one game against New Zealand and would have liked the chance of many more. I found New Zealand to be a superbly drilled team, highly efficient in all aspects, and ten times more assured when they are going forward than if you put them on the back foot. The All Blacks are the noisiest international team as well, always chattering at the referee about how they see this and that, so much so you have to assume it is deliberate policy. Australia, who play the All Blacks more than anybody, have similar characteristics.

All these countries, together with South Africa, who have been in, out, and now back in world rugby, formed the old hard core of the international game. They ran rugby and it was their show, and for years that situation persisted until the revolution caught up with that cartel as well. England could not be blamed for that because the Rugby Union has been in the forefront of expanding the game for 20 years or more, and Fiji came here on tour for the Rugby Union centenary.

The Fijians were mystery men from the South Pacific in those days but have gone from being a team which could worry anybody to seven-a-side specialists and little else.

The revolution at international level came in the shape of the World Cup. The event was kick-started by Australia and New Zealand in 1987, when they jointly hosted the first competition. The World Cup might not have been received with total enthusiasm by the home countries but that very first event showed everyone where they stood in relation to New Zealand. In terms of fitness and match-planning the All Blacks led the way. I was one of the England World Cup squad in 1987, but as the management of the day chose not to pick me for a single match I did feel slightly on the outside. But I shared the gloom when England were beaten in the quarter-finals by Wales and could sense from the inquests the next day that England were going to go full bore to make their mark in the World Cup. Four years later, of course, we were the beaten finalists against Australia at Twickenham and this time I am glad to say that I did play my part.

The World Cup has influenced so much, and if England were a little slow off the mark, a little reluctant to join the party, you would have to agree that they made valiant efforts to catch up. The changes have been enormous, starting with the introduction of a team manager, a job previously carried out by a chairman of selectors. Mike Weston was the first manager, appointed in 1985 to take us to the World Cup in 1987. Later that year Geoff Cooke succeeded him and inherited a squad of players which included some very experienced men who gave him the foundation to build a team which won back-to-back Grand Slams in the Five Nations' Championship in 1991 and 1992 – and reached the World Cup final.

Cooke was the first manager to choose me for the England side. I owe my first 37 caps to his selection. Against that I am convinced that he wanted me out of the side on other occasions and particularly after the end of the 1992 Championship – which made it all the more gratifying to me to come back in again in 1993. Cooke was also the first manager to pin long-term faith in one player as captain when he named Carling in 1988 as the man to lead the England side through to the 1991 World Cup. It has turned out to be an even longer appointment than that and has made Carling a unique figure in English rugby. He has taken the commercial opportunities open to him with both hands, and the more he is selected, presumably the greater those opportunities will become.

Money in the game has been another part of the revolution – the biggest and most contentious part if you listen to some members of the Rugby Union committee, as I have. They claim that it is total anathema to them that any player should receive any kind of financial reward for anything to do with the game. This is how it was in their day and how they see it now. The England players have a counter-argument that the time arrived some while ago for them to be able to make money from off-the-field promotional activities. That scheme came into place in World Cup year, 1991, and after a bad start, with heavy losses, has paid out some money. It is nothing that will change your life but there was a pay out. Future England squads may benefit from the foundations laid by the players of my era. Where we go next I cannot predict, but there will be more movement because the pace is being set in the Southern Hemisphere by the Australians and New Zealanders who have set up well-documented and broadly based schemes for the benefit of their players. At the same time the Rugby Union is trying to clamp down on the suggestions that the game in England is already semi-professional and that players are being paid at many levels. There is too much conflict here for that situation to last for ever. We ask for a level playing field to play our rugby. Before the next World Cup the England squad will be asking the Rugby Union for a level playing field in all aspects of commercialism, I am convinced of that.

The players are not alone in reacting to the new commercialism in the game. Everyone wants money. Clubs want sponsors – and those sponsors want to be associated with success which creates its own pressure to filter down to the players. Counties and divisions in England want sponsors who again want to be associated with success. The Rugby Union itself needs sponsors to support its competitions and general development as well as run the twenty-first century stadium which Twickenham is becoming. In my time Twickenham has gone from being a cosy old-fashioned stadium with a south terrace, a north stand, and its two east and west stands, which have been the backdrop of thousands of photographs, to what it is now – one last piece of development short of complete change. Successful and successive England teams have helped to create the financial stability for these changes to take place.

Everything which has happened since 1987 has put England on a higher plane, a target for everyone, particularly in the Five Nations Championship. Wales seem to have gone back to the view that if they can beat England, as they did in 1993, then nothing else matters. They beat us 10–9 and then slumped for the rest of the Championship. Ireland caught us in their final game and played with a rare fury all the way through – but would they have produced such sustained drive against anyone else? It really makes me wonder. Historically, England have been the playing enemy of so many. Now we have to live up to the high standards we have set over the past few years and that will mean more organisation, more time away from home and work, and more demands from the players for a slice of the cake. Whatever is thought to be abnormal this year will become natural for next year's players and the equation will move on from there.

One way to judge that rugby union players are being taken care of more these days is that any movement to rugby league has virtually dried up. Very few English players have felt the need to move over anyway and Wales took care of their last big name to threaten to move, Scott Gibbs, by creating a financial package which kept him at home. The Australians and New Zealanders are producing their financial plans with the intent of halting any drift to rugby league by their players. I hasten to add that no rugby league team has made me an offer and is unlikely to now. But with my ball-handling skills I would not have been out of place!

As I say, some people might think I have made an impossible journey but it has never seemed like that to me. I have had more satisfaction than setbacks and I hope there is more satisfaction to come. One of the spin-offs of the England regime has been greatly improved fitness and stamina levels, and I do not intend to slacken off. I feel now that it will not be beyond me to play First Division rugby at the age of 40 but I will be taking things a season at a time like a number of props who have been knocking around the game in England as long as I have – Paul Rendall, Gareth Chilcott, Gary Pearce, and Sammy Southern among them.

My one regret is that I have not toured with the British Lions. I was injured during the critical selection time for the 1989 tour to Australia and not chosen for the 1993 trip to New Zealand. The rest of the England pack went and I was the lone exclusion. Many people said I should have gone before the tour started and many more said I should have gone once the squad returned. Geoff Cooke, who managed the tour, wrote to me and said that for me it had come a year too late, which was little consolation. Even I accept that by 1997, the year when the Lions travel again, that I will be out of the reckoning! I leave the final comment on the Lions selection to Mark Bailey, my colleague from Wasps and England, who, in his Rugby Union Commentary in *The Daily Telegraph*, said the following:

> As the dust settles over the selection for the Lions' tour to New Zealand, let us be grateful that the tour management have been allowed to pick their squad free from the regresssive influences of national tokenism.
>
> The result is a record–equalling 16 Englishmen but only two Irishmen; a welcome return for Dean Richards, but no Back, no Probyn, and ominously for the squad's flexibility – no Robert Jones.
>
> The management have nailed the colours of their playing strategy firmly to the mast. This is a monolithic pack, but monoliths are not noted for their pace around a rugby field. As New Zealand are unlikely to pass through this set of Lions forwards we must also hope that they fail to outmanoeuvre them.
>
> The absence of Jeffrey Probyn is baffling given his performance this season. Some Irish players reckoned that Probyn was the only English forward to withstand their whirlwind at Lansdowne Road and many rate him among the best props in the world. England made a mistake when they dropped Probyn against South Africa and the Lions have done the same.
>
> Probyn can regard himself as very unlucky. At 36 he is the venerable Mr Blobby of the England team: zestful, talkative, endearing, sometimes mischievous and involved in an ambivalent relationship with Will Carling and the management. He remains commendably sanguine

about his omission from the Lions, regarding the news as 'a bitter pill to swallow: but one made sweeter by the respect of my peers'. The knowledge that he is held in the highest esteem by those he plays against may temper Probyn's disappointment but it will also fuel his disbelief.

A measure of Probyn's rating in the dark world of front-row play was indicated during one club match in the late 1980s. After the game Probyn's face was puffy and florid, the result of receiving the undivided attention of the opposite pack for a full 80 minutes. When asked why Probyn had been singled out for such intensive treatment, his opposing prop replied with a mixture of awe and candour: 'Wasps are only likely to beat us if Probyn was allowed to concentrate on his scrummaging – so we took the precaution of distracting him.'

Another feature of Probyn's career has been his physical resilience. He prefers playing the game to training and plays whenever he can. And, unlike many props battered by international rugby, his malleable body is not injury-prone. Wasps once faced Bath in a Merit Table decider with the backbone of their pack ruled out by injury. Probyn had undergone key-hole surgery on his knee two weeks previously and the thought of taking on the mighty Bath pack with an assortment of green youngsters would not have appealed to many established stars. Despite a highly respectable excuse, the option of withdrawing from the team did not even occur to Probyn. The Bath forwards were rampant, the green youngsters wilted and Probyn was in constant discomfort from his knee. Yet when Bath scored a pushover try from a scrum he neither looked for excuses nor offered any.

Every rugby club has a Jeffrey Probyn, one immensely tough and selfless character who is utterly dependable. Few players, however, retain all these characteristics when they become established internationals. Yet, for the past four years, England have been fortunate to possess a core of similar characters, from Probyn to Dooley to Ackford, Teague, Richards and Winterbottom.

Let there be no doubt that England's unparalleled success in recent seasons has been primarily constructed upon the efforts and abilities of these core players. After the humbling in Ireland, Will Carling was right to emphasise that they must be remembered for their immense contribution to this success.

All of which sounds like a valediction to Jeff Probyn and, in a sense, it is. He is the only one among England's ageing giants to be denied a fitting farewell in New Zealand. Probyn cannot have been omitted from the Lions because of his age or his physical ability to last an eight-week tour. He cannot have been omitted on the grounds of immobility because the Lions have selected a set-piece pack. Perhaps his line-out work is deemed to lack sufficient craft or caper. If Jeffrey Probyn wasn't such a philosophical or such an articulate man, he might confess to feeling as sick as a parrot.

Chapter Two

MY NAUTICAL CONNECTION

The Probyn family has been around the East End of London for a long time. I can claim a little French descent because my great-grandfather was married to a French parlourmaid and my own father, Charles, comes from that line. My grandfather Albert was a furniture manufacturer – the plaque from his working days hangs on my office wall – and my Dad started our present business 40 years ago. My mum, Pat, produced my brother Chris 18 months before me and I weighed in on 27 April 1956, at 9lbs 9oz at Bethnal Green Hospital. We had a close-knit family life based on the village atmosphere which you could find in any street in the East End. Even the Angel at Islington seemed a far-off place in those days. It was a surprise if you met someone from that distance.

I was born injured because the surgeon who performed the Caesarean section cut a little piece out of my left ear which blended in nicely with all the other lumps and bumps I was to acquire later in life. But I have maintained an association with the Bethnal Green Hospital in later years and do what I can to help their activities. I have also stayed in the East End to live and work – I married my wife Jennifer in 1975 and we have three children. Jeffrey was born in 1976, Steven in 1977, and Rebecca in 1980. Steven, so far, is the only one of my children to want to play rugby and it will not surprise you to know that he is playing prop.

For the first 11 years of my life I lived at 90 New North Road in a three-storey town house which has since been pulled down. We moved along the road to real luxury because next we had central heating and a bath in the house. I was a pupil at Burbage School which had a concrete playground but no organised sport other than what the kids put together themselves. I don't remember any impromptu games of rugby – you have to remember I lived in what was essentially a soccer area with Arsenal, Tottenham, and West Ham all very close. The plan for me at the time was to go through school and take up a trade, which is what happened, but by passing the 11-plus examination I unwittingly set myself on the road to playing rugby. My brother was already ahead of me at the London Nautical School, south of the River Thames in Stamford Street between Blackfriars and Waterloo bridges, and once I passed that exam I was on the way to join him. The horizons of life suddenly broadened. Soon it would be the 76 or 141 London Transport bus to and from school, and I would be leaving Burbage behind.

I never made the soccer team at Burbage and my memory says I have been to only two soccer games in my life. I went to watch Spurs play Manchester United with my mate Freddy. It was the first time I had been in a big crowd and I didn't see much. I also went to Chelsea with my mate Brian Plummer. It was at the time when Peter Osgood was playing for Chelsea and it's funny how that 'Osgood is Good' chant sticks in your mind after all those years. I played a little five-a-side soccer and snooker and put in some rifle shooting and once I boxed for the Crown and Manor Club. I knocked my opponent out but he got up and carried on and I won on points. I never boxed again.

The London Nautical School under John Allott, its headmaster when I began, had a policy of not only educating you but making you more worldly wise. Even though it was in the heart of London it was a Surrey school. Our playing fields were out at Morden, and it was there that I had my first touch of a rugby ball. It was one of those big old brown leather things, very heavy when it hit you, and I wondered what it was all about. I had my first pair of boots to play with, good old-fashioned boots with a toe cap and cork studs. I could have had the best gear in the world for all the difference it made to the sports master Brian Dixon who clearly felt I had zero potential for the game. In Brian's considered view I was absolutely useless, would never be any good at rugby as long as I lived, and had no aptitude and no attitude for the game. For that first year, you will understand, I did not quite make the team.

But things improved. Another master, a Mr Bulby, had more faith in my untapped abilities and showed more enthusiasm. I was in with a bunch of miscreants at the time, but he told me that because I was short and fat I might as well try playing at hooker. We practised and it must have gone reasonably well for me because I was promoted to the first team for the rest of the season. The following season I found that I had grown taller than my props which would not have helped our balance in the front row and I went to prop instead, at loose-head. The school was starting to make a reputation as a place which produced rugby players and I had a family target to follow because my brother had already won selection for the London Counties under-15 team. In my fourth year I made the Surrey trials for the first time, played three of the four planned 20-minute periods, scored two tries, and was replaced by Ed Horne who went on to play three university matches for Oxford.

Finally I reached the London side, still playing at loose-head, and looking back I realise that selection for that level meant they saw me as the best prop from a considerable area of the country. I was just happy to play anywhere and for anybody in those days – I once guested for Wandsworth School on a tour but offered to play centre because I did not want to disrupt their regular front row. I suppose I was a bit of a loner looking for a game because there was nowhere around where I lived where I could go.

Life at the London Nautical School was literally a nautical existence. I attended daily in my sailor-suit uniform, Second Starboard was my school house, and we lined up each day for inspection to make

27

sure we were clean and presentable and did not need a haircut or our shoes cleaning. I took my O-level examinations in navigation and seamanship. Each year we had a Viking camp, sailing on the Isle of Sheppey in a dinghy from which fortunately no one was ever lost. I learned to sail a drop-keel boat. I rowed clinker-built boats in the Surrey Docks, and studied Morse code and boat construction in order to understand strength and durability. The aim was to prepare boys for entry to the Merchant Navy, which I never took up, but it was all good experience.

In rugby I continued to have the target set by my brother to aim at. He was a sporting hero to me, and it was only when I made the London team that I actually went past him. He is a prop as well so he knows what it is all about but he is more talkative and makes more noise. He is also a black belt in judo, works in the London financial market, and if you come across him these days he might be playing for Redbridge.

Eventually I captained the school team. We had an unbeaten season for the first time, which meant we had to beat schools like St Joseph's College, St Benedict's, and Rossall as well as win the annual match with our nautical colleagues at Dartmouth. I was chosen for an England schools trial, played at Beckenham, but I was very nervous, under-performed and did not progress. Some of the bigger clubs were already taking an interest in me – Harlequins made an approach, for instance – but my first step into a higher grade of rugby came while I was still at school and took me to Old Albanians in St Albans.

One of the masters at the London Nautical School was Nicko Brandt, at that time a supply teacher who took us for religious education and helped out with rugby coaching. He went on to become a barrister and circuit judge in Essex but it was he who persuaded me to play for Albanians. I don't know whether John Brand, our PE teacher at the time and now headmaster, was aware that some of us were playing for the school in the morning and then went off to Albanians in the afternoon. That is what we did but I have to say that the London Nautical School played a considerable part in my development in rugby and John Brand knows that I have recognised that by giving them one of my England shirts. I believe I am the only international rugby player to come through the school which saddens me in a way because there must be an untapped market of boys in inner London who deserve their chance at rugby. It was an educational accident that introduced me to the game. Now rugby has to work much harder to recruit youngsters and I would welcome any initiative which penetrates the hearts of our major cities.

My twice-a-day routine continued while I was at school and suited me down to the ground. I was a young lad being introduced to the world of senior rugby and the thrill I got out of going to Beech Bottom, that leafy old-style ground in St Albans, was considerable. That was not my only rugby because a school-friend, Phil Cochrane, lived in Ilford and was captain of their colts team. I had occasional games with them as well and probably played everywhere except prop. The last game I played for Ilford, aged 17, was also my shortest because I was sent off when I punched someone who had punched me. I never found out if I was suspended or not, so I played on.

At Albanians I was introduced to a player and captain named Darryl Druce. He had played for Coventry and knew his stuff and at that level was a brilliant tight-head prop. He remembers me arriving there with my brother around 1973 and turning out in the lower teams at centre. He knew I was not really a centre but he liked the way I used to run through everybody to score. Darryl says he told a lot of people I was going to play for England, and of course it took 13 years for his views to be justified. I was the top try-scorer one season and was enjoying myself totally in what was a new world for me but I knew I wanted to try again at prop and not be a centre. I spoke to Darryl about it and he said: 'Just see how far you can go, just try it, and if you make it, great.'

The switch worked. I made the Albanians front row and played with Darryl and hooker Steve John for a couple of seasons. Darryl remembers:

Jeff's first game in the first team was against Hampstead who always had a smattering of Australian and New Zealand players. That day it was said around our dressing-room that they had an Australian who had played against the All Blacks in the Bledisloe Cup, the trophy competed for annually by New Zealand and Australia. It was also said they had this guy who was a bit of a gorilla and that after a while there was a bit of a squabble between the gorilla and this young athlete called Probyn, that there were two thuds and some blood in the tunnel of the scrum, and I said to myself that young Jeff was taking care of things.

I was still with Albanians when I played a game for Hertfordshire against Buckinghamshire, and Gary Pearce, who had just been capped by England for the first time at the age of 23, was in the opposition. I was not actually qualified for Hertfordshire but somebody had contrived a Hertfordshire address for me and I played for them quite happily – and also later on for both Surrey and Middlesex. I had a tough match against Pearce and my fellow prop suggested I moved over to tight-head, which did him no good at all. This was in a second-team match, an evening game at Hertford, and I never made it up to the first team.

I also knew it was time to move on if I was to prove anything further to myself about my abilities. I had learned a great deal at Albanians in a style of rugby which was basically a static mauling game full of gnarled, experienced men who I enjoyed running through for tries. I liked to set off from tap penalties or line-out peels and see what I could do with what was called my ramrod hand-off, and I found I was getting away with it more and more. Albanians knew of my ambitions and we parted amicably. It meant saying goodbye in playing terms to my brother and a lot of mates in the Albanians pack. Much later, when I made the England bench for the first time, I gave that shirt to Nicko Brandt because I knew how much influence he had had on my career at that early stage. The next stop was at Streatham–Croydon in Thornton Heath, South London.

I knew a lot about Streatham. I had a few friends down there and to me it was a logical move. I had managed to pop their tight-head prop out of a scrum or two when I had played against them but I began there at loose-head. In the second season I moved to hooker because the first choice was injured, won two or three strikes against the head in a match with the Chicago Lions and enjoyed the experience. Surrey Clubs picked me at prop that season and when Streatham had an injury at prop I moved across to tight-head for the first time on a serious basis.

This conformed exactly with the thinking of the Streatham front-row expert Dennis Bedford who believed all along that I would never be big enough to play higher up at loose-head but that I was perfectly equipped for the other side of the front row. I still wasn't sure because everywhere I had played at loose-head I had made the first team. When I played against so-called better teams I had found that the pace was up, often phenomenally so, but that I was able to cope. And when I did move I had a bit of a reputation to take with me but I still felt it was important to stick with people that I liked. So I stayed at Streatham for close to four years until, out of the blue, Richmond came looking for me.

Dennis Bedford was appraised of what I was doing. He told me straight that I was the best tight-head prop he had ever seen and not to change positions any more. From what I understood from Richmond, they were in dire straits for any kind of prop and guaranteed me a second-team place. I was now 25 and the prospect of moving up the scale a little more appealed to me. Richmond were a big club then with a big fixture list and I saw the move as further progress. They put me in the third team to start me off (which hardly coincided with their promise) and the first game was against Rochford 100. Tony Bucknall, the former England captain, led the side and I suppose he was scouting to see what I could do. The next week I went up to the second team and in that first season with Richmond I was in the first team 15 times. I also knew at the end of that season that tight-head was for me. I remembered Bedford's advice and I was not going to change from tight-head. A few games in the so-called top rung of the day were enough to convince me.

Richmond brought me into closer contact with Chris Ralston. People say he is lugubrious but to me he is a big bloke with long hair and a deep voice who smokes a lot and has been through a few major tests with England and the British Lions. I had half a dozen games with him in the Richmond seconds – he was technically on the way down at the time – and much useful information passed between us with him in the second row and me at prop. Ralston, at that stage, was the most experienced forward I had played with and he told me what was required of me in the line-out and scrum. I believe I was present when

31

Ralston played his final game on a mudheap pitch at Finchley. It rained throughout the game and we had to wait for 15 minutes outside the dressing-room afterwards until someone found the key. Chris stayed in his sodden kit, decided to drive home, and as far as I know was never seen in a Richmond shirt again.

I had two more full seasons with Richmond, 19 games in the first year, 23 in the second. I scored four tries for the first team. Middlesex had tried me but were very Harlequins orientated then and chose Terry Claxton at prop after I thought I had played well for them against the British Police. Surrey offered me a chance which I took. All this meant that by the summer of 1984 I was playing regularly in Richmond's first team and regularly for Surrey. I was not unhappy with that state of affairs. I felt I was fulfilling myself. It was now a question of seeing what came next.

Chapter Three

THE CALL OF WASPS

My target at the start of the 1984–85 season was to win a place in the London division squad. The previous season, under Maurice Colclough's captaincy, they had run the New Zealand tourists close, 18–15, at Twickenham and there was a mood of optimism among the London players that they could do the same or better against the Australians who were due next. England had gone one better than London in 1983 by beating New Zealand at Twickenham 15–9 for the first home win over the All Blacks since 1936. But the follow-up in the 1984 Championship had been disappointing with just one win, against Ireland. And when England went to South Africa on a close-season tour, the last contact they had with them for eight years, they were thumped in both Tests.

London provided the first opponents to the Australians who were the last tourists to have the opportunity to win a Grand Slam against all four home countries, which they duly did. Since then a maximum of two countries appear on tour fixture lists and the chance which those Australians took so well is no longer there. I cleared another playing hurdle when London chose me for the squad but I did not win a place in the team – that went to Simon Henderson of Rosslyn Park. I was brought in to scrummage against the London pack along with John Olver and Paul Essenhigh, and when we started to push them around and embarrass them Colclough sent a few shots through from the London second row to remind us of who was meant to be in control. Wasps had eight players in the final selection, indicating their role as London club team of the time.

I had always wanted to go on to Twickenham in a representative game and my chance came after an hour when Paul Curtis was injured. I think we had the nudge on the Aussie pack once or twice after I came on but there was no way the eventual result was going to alter. Australia won 22–3 and it is interesting to reflect now that four of their young players in that game, David Campese, Nick Farr-Jones, Michael Lynagh, and Simon Poidevin, all came through to the World Cup final against England seven years later. Paul Ackford and I from the London side were the only players who could claim the same distinction. The Aussie side was solid that winter – it ran through all four English divisions and beat England 19–3.

After the London match the first overtures were made to me about moving to Wasps from Richmond. I have always believed that players are the best recruiting agents for clubs and here was Alan Simmons, the Wasps and London hooker, explaining to me that Wasps were looking for a tight-head prop and that I was the man for the job. I had seen myself that Wasps had three men in the London pack, and that was not counting Paul Rendall who missed the Australian game. If I was going to progress this was a logical move and I told Richmond that I was leaving because I felt it would help my England ambitions to try my hand with Wasps. Richmond were quite vitriolic about the move and there were murmurs of cheque-book recruitment – but I am still waiting for the day when someone will offer, let alone pay for me to move clubs. As there was no Courage League in those days and no need for player registration as exists now, players could move when and where they wanted. So I went – after just eight games for Richmond in the early part of that season.

I anticipated I would be more on display at Wasps than Richmond, provided I could win a place in the first team where there was plenty of experience with Rendall and Simmons in the front row, and Colclough, Keith Bonner, David Pegler and Keith Moss behind them. Rendall and Colclough were England players and Simmons was a B player. After I had been in the second team for a match or two – and been told that I might be a decent prop but my foot positioning was all wrong – I made it into the first team. Wasps, under Nigel Melville's captaincy and Alan Black's coaching, played to a pattern and knew what they were doing. We had proof of that, too, in the first Rugby Union approved merit tables where we finished top of the ten-club London division. It was a bit of a farce because only two clubs managed to fulfil nine fixtures and Harlequins only played four. But it gave the season a little more bite. Wasps were deserving winners in London while Bath won the South-West, Sale topped the North, and Nottingham came through as best in the Midlands.

My move to Wasps confirmed my belief that the best teams come under more scrutiny. It was a place to be seen alright, but it did not mean that I started moving towards the England side at a rate of knots. Gary Pearce, who had moved to Northampton from Aylesbury, had the tight-head spot against Australia and stayed on for the rest of the season against Romania at Twickenham – where England capped Wade Dooley and Rob Andrew for the first time – and then into the Championship.

Nobody down south knew much about Dooley. He was playing with Preston Grasshoppers which meant he did not come into contact with most of the big clubs. Some of us remembered him running on for the North as a replacement against Romania at Birkenhead Park and only one week later he was in the England team. He missed out on a couple of matches in that first year but was to become first choice all the way through to 1993. Wade is a year younger than me and did not win his first cap until he was 27 – and that selection showed that England had room for the more mature player.

Wasps did not have the impact on the 1985 England team which might have been anticipated. Simon Smith played on the wing all the way through and Melville was chosen twice. But that was it for my new colleagues at Sudbury. England started off with a draw against France 9–9 and beat Scotland 10–7 but were remarkably fortunate not to lose both games. Patrick Esteve delayed a touchdown for France and had the ball knocked from his hands in goal and Iain Paxton was robbed of the ball in a similar piece of play by Scotland. Defeats followed against Ireland and Wales – and England still had to face a tour to New Zealand with two Tests against the All Blacks.

Dick Greenwood, who had been England coach for two years and had played a major part in Dooley's development, was not available so Martin Green, a former Cambridge University captain and at that stage the under-23 coach, took over in an appointment that was to last beyond the first World Cup in 1987. England also used Brian Ashton as backs coach, the first time they had taken two coaches on a tour. I knew I was not in the frame for selection – Pearce and Austin Sheppard of Bristol were the tight-head choices – and it sounded like a good tour to miss. New Zealand won the first Test 18–13 and the second by a record score of 42–15.

The next target for me was the Divisional Championship, re-introduced in 1985, and Wasps really did gain some recognition this time with six men in the pack and four in the backs. We stopped the South-West 22–3 and pulled off a critical 7–3 win over the North at Otley. The North fancied their chances on one of their favourite grounds and Melville, playing against us, would never have stopped reminding us if the North had won. Unfortunately the Midlands mauled us out of the title in the last game 12–3.

The 1986 Championship was the first under the new management team of Mike Weston and Martin Green who were appointed to take England through to the World Cup. It started well with Rob Andrew scoring all the points in the 21–18 win over Wales but went wrong in a big way at Murrayfield against Scotland. The Scots have never had it so good, winning by a record 33–6 with Gavin Hastings making his mark with 21 points, and suddenly England were back at base camp. Weston made front-row and back-row changes and Dean Richards made his debut at number eight against Ireland. There was heavy frost in the week of the game but the Twickenham ground staff won their particular battle against the weather and the match was played on a bone-hard ground. Richards had a marvellous day with two tries from pushovers. He should have had a hat trick but Ireland kicked the ball away from him as he was about to drop on it – and conceded a penalty try as a result. Richards could not have asked for or provided a stronger start to his international career and went on to be at the core of so many important England performances. England won that game 25–20 in such cold conditions that the players actually went off the field at half-time to warm themselves. England's final game against France in Paris ended in a 29–10 win for the French – and the World Cup was now only a year away. England looked nowhere near ready to take the step into the unknown.

With Wasps I was still enjoying myself. The merit tables took on more meaning in 1985–86 because they were conducted on a national basis and Wasps finished third, behind Gloucester and Nottingham. In the more meaningful competition at that time, the John Player Cup, we reached the final at Twickenham against Bath which brought me into personal battle with Gareth 'Cooch' Chilcott who had played for England in the last two games of the Championship and was right on song.

We thought that Bath would create a few difficulties for us and resolved to play the final with an element of surprise and counter-attack at every opportunity. This worked like a dream and we were 13–nil up after 25 minutes. We had two tries in three minutes from Nick Stringer and Roger Pellow who topped off a move which started way back in our own 22. Richard Cardus, the Yorkshireman who captained us at centre, and our New Zealand coach Derek Arnold insisted we kept the game free and adventurous, and Bath were obviously upset by our tactics.

But Bath had walked the Twickenham route before. Wasps started the game without Rendall, who had measles, and our scrum-half Steve Bates went off late in the first half with a broken arm. On top of that Bath began to put some real vigour and organisation into their forward drives and came back to win 25–17, four tries to three. We very much wanted to be the first London club to win the Cup in its 15-year history and it was little consolation that we were the first beaten finalists to score three tries.

We had had a hectic run in to Twickenham. The competition was hit that year by bad weather which left us to play and win three matches in 15 days to make the final. The most controversial was the middle one of the three against Nottingham on their ground at Beeston. The Rugby Union ordered this game to be played on Good Friday after a long sequence of discussion between the two clubs. The match finished 13–13 and what took us through to the semi-finals was a try eight minutes from the end by Mark Bailey who chased a big diagonal kick by Gareth Rees, our 18-year-old fly-half from Harrow School who has since become Canada's number ten. We then took out London Scottish 11–3 in the semi-final.

England took a development squad to Italy for two games – we managed to draw the unofficial test 11–11 against Italy in Rome. I played in Sicily and that gave me my first playing experience with Brian Moore at hooker, neither of us realising that we were about to start a lengthy playing relationship two years later. The England hooker in possession in 1986 was Steve Brain, then of Coventry, and it would be fair to say that his ideas on fitness and training did not exactly coincide with the management which was trying to persuade a squad of around 50 players to change their ways in preparation for the World Cup. We went to Portugal for a training camp which meant running through the pine forests on the Algarve and on the beaches, and putting in some carefully planned work on the running track and in the gym. Green, who knew Brain as well as anyone, spent a long time drilling the values of fitness into the hooker. Brain listened to it all but would say afterwards: 'It's a load of crap. Just put everyone in a scrum with me and let's see who is left at the end.' But England never picked him again.

The training camps in Portugal brought us into contact with Tom McNab, the former AAA national coach. Tom is a very voluble Scot and clearly knew the track-and-field business inside out. Later, when we moved our warm-weather training from Portugal to Lanzarote where many athletes were in residence, Tom could switch from one sport to the other without drawing breath, always offering advice. But in those first sessions he showed us how he wanted us to run which may sound simple but a good many players, myself included, had to look again at what we thought was running and see how far adrift it was from Tom's methods. I had always thought I was fairly quick over the ground and the testing proved that. With Tom I upped the pace a little as well.

Tom was scathing of the general athleticism of the front row men but told us that the hookers were better than the props. The backs came out of the whole exercise with high marks, especially Rory Underwood who could throw the shot almost to Olympic standard. McNab wanted us all to concentrate on improving our speed, as well as our body power to make us more effective in the tackle and maul, our stamina to recover quickly after maximum effort, and our strength to fix our scrum positions. All this was new ground back in 1986 but has become an accepted part of the game today, honed and refined to even higher levels. Today's shape of player contrasts vividly with that of a few years ago. Where have the beer bellies gone?

Weston, as manager, was concerned with improving the image of England players by introducing official clothing for all games instead of just tours, as had been the case. He put in demands for improvements in the allocation of tickets for England players for matches at Twickenham, set up dental and physiotherapy back-up, and suggested the installation of a scrummage machine next to the England dressing-room at Twickenham was a sound idea. It was, and still is, just for setting the scrum and feeling comfortable about what we are doing in the time before we go out and play.

Japan, who were one of our World Cup pool opponents in 1987, played an England team at Twickenham in the autumn of 1986. Richard Hill of Bath was made captain for the first time and Bath dominated the selection with six players. Moore emerged at hooker, propped by Chilcott and Pearce, and after a first half which saw Japan lead 12–6 England pulled themselves round and won 39–12.

The Divisional Championship followed, and when London started off against the Midlands it was almost like a Wasps' home game – played on our ground at Sudbury and with everyone in the side a member of Wasps with the exception of Jamie Salmon of Harlequins at centre and Simon Smith of Richmond at fly-half. These two scored all the points as well in our 13–9 win but after that we lost 11–nil to the South-West, and then, back at Wasps, were beaten 34–6 by the North. I guessed correctly that I had not done my chances much good because in the England trial at the start of 1987 the tight-head props were Pearce and Bath's Richard Lee.

World Cup year started badly for England – and I was able to see it at first hand against Ireland in Dublin. We were missing Dooley and Steve Bainbridge from the second row but that was just the start of our troubles. Ireland took their customary playing style to the limits, thanks to the French referee Renee Hourquet, and won in something of a canter by 17–nil. In such an important year, it was a disaster.

I came off that bench and into the England B team to play France at Bath on a Friday night – the day before the Championship game. The selectors had given Mark Bailey a good-looking side to captain with experienced forwards in every row: Simmons alongside me, Nigel Redman at lock, Micky Skinner and Andy Robinson on the flanks. Peter Williams of Orrell was the fly-half and he had Fran Clough and Carling at centre, Bailey and Chris Oti on the wings, Jon Webb at full-back. Alan Davies was coach and he asked us all how we wanted to play and let us formulate our own game plan. It was a different approach for many of us, relaxed but still concentrated, and the only thing which was crossing my mind was how to cope with French intimidation on what promised to be a volatile evening under the Recreation Ground floodlights.

It was open warfare from the start. Marocco, the French prop, was not at all pleased at being dropped from their Championship side and objected when we took two or three strikes against the head. There was a lot of heavy rucking whenever you hit the ground and punches galore in the front row, so much so that Simmons could hardly see through his swollen eyes. Skinner loved it and was putting in big hits all over the place in the manner to which France would later become accustomed on an even bigger stage. We scored a couple of tries in our 22–9 win which was roared on by as appreciative a crowd as you could hope to run out for. The atmosphere was marvellous and when we scored our last try from a 15-metre scrum you knew what was going to happen. Both French second-row men came punching through as the scrum broke up and there was quite a battle between both sets of forwards as the try was being put in. If I remember rightly, only a couple of French players turned up at the post-match reception.

It was as a benchmark for each player in that B side because we had imposed our will on a match where we could so easily have been swept aside. The vibrations lived on for some time afterwards.

England played France at Twickenham the next day. France won that 19–15 but of greater significance to me was the injury to Rendall after just 12 minutes. Chilcott subbed for him but the injury was severe enough for Rendall to be ruled out of the side to play Wales in Cardiff. Chilcott stayed in and I was on the bench for the first time. I knew all about the historical significance of going to Wales, that England's last win had been in 1963, and there were all the usual threats on either side about how tense it was going to be. The attitude in the England dressing-room was quite clear to me – no one was going to take a backward step. If one of our forwards was under attack the rest should act. Green reminded us that Wales would do everything to maintain their record over England at Cardiff. Richard Hill, captain in a Championship match for the third time, laid it on the line that we had to come away with a win after all the humiliations which previous England teams, many of them solid ones, had suffered. It was definitely firework time as I made my way to the bench. The key confrontation of the game was to take place right in front of me.

The root of all the trouble was Bob Norster's elbow. In only the second line-out Norster had aimed his elbow at Steve Bainbridge and succeeded in hitting his own team mate, Steve Sutton, fracturing his nose. This prompted a fair old fist-fight and Dooley, reacting to a punch on Jon Hall, laid into Phil Davies and broke his cheekbone. Strangely enough, when you considered all the Welsh whingeing afterwards, the referee, Ray Megson of Scotland, awarded a penalty against Wales when he restarted play but the incident hung over England for the rest of the game, the rest of the season, and on until they were beaten by Wales in the World Cup three months later. Wales won the match 19–12 and all sorts of people got stuck into England afterwards as if we were the only ones to create trouble. A lot of holier-than-thou views came out of the woodwork and Dooley was under considerable pressure at the post-match dinner and later on when the fact that he was a policeman led to a lengthy trial by newsprint. When I looked at the replay it confirmed my view that Dooley should not have retaliated on Hall's behalf but it had happened. The Rugby Union banned four players for one game – Dooley, Chilcott, who was no angel but had done nothing wrong, hooker Graham Dawe on the video evidence rather than first hand, and Hill, the captain. Dooley took it all on the chin and recovered his place quickly. Chilcott faded after 1989 and Dawe played one more game. Hill came back to command a regular place in 1990. Wales, publicly, found nothing wrong with the behaviour of any of their players on the pitch that day.

The England management reacted to the Rugby Union request, and more, because they took the opportunity for the final game before the World Cup of leaving out Rob Andrew, and giving a first game to Peter Williams, and also leaving out Peter Winterbottom. Mike Harrison, the Wakefield and Yorkshire wing, was made captain and all the team had to do now was stop Scotland winning the Triple Crown at Twickenham. It was an ideal backs-to-the-wall situation for England and the response from the forwards was so good that Scotland were beaten 21–12 and could have gone down by a lot more. All that was left for the selectors to do was finalise the squad for the World Cup and they chose the team which beat Scotland en bloc – minus Simon Halliday who was not available – together with another 11 players, including myself. The four who had been left out on disciplinary grounds were reinstated but the captaincy remained with Harrison. I could not argue with the front-row choices – Rendall, Pearce, Chilcott and me were the props, Moore and Dawe were the hookers.

Wasps were still in the John Player Cup, heading for the Twickenham final for a second year, once more to play Bath. Wasps had slipped in the merit table to ninth place but this was the last season of the hit-and-miss fixture arrangements of that time: the following season a nationwide league involving more than 1,200 clubs was to come into operation, sowing the seeds for the huge competition we have today. Our Cup run in 1987 started at Rugby but we then had three home ties to make Twickenham. We beat Midland clubs all the way – Rugby, Nottingham, Coventry and Leicester – and once again, with few changes in personnel, it was Bath and a 35,000 crowd at Twickenham – just ten days before we were due to fly out to Australia for the World Cup.

The final brought me up against David Sole for the first important test between us. Others were to follow when we came to grips for England and Scotland but we went into that final with points to make and I believe I came out of that one on top because Sole complained afterwards that he had concussion. Bath had always recognised that scrummaging was not Sole's forte. He was a very good player around the park but scrummaging was something he had to work on. Roger Spurrell, who had been captain of Bath, told me before that final that they had warned Sole to watch out for Probyn and he had said something along the lines of 'Don't worry, I can handle him.' Spurrell had explained to Sole about my technique where I looked to turn the loose-head upward, put pressure on him, and create situations where he does not know if he is coming or going. Go high, go low, strike or don't strike for the ball, or push or take a push, with me dictating the terms. A top loose-head will have his own game plan to counteract you and the thing often evens out, leaving you looking for small advantages. Many times in practice I have been down to an inch above the grass and come up again under full control. It was something I could do over and over again in one-on-one training situations with Rendall. You can do it in a match as well as long as everyone around is aware of what is going on but I would not recommend it for fun. I heard that Spurrell took the rise out of Sole after the final and I felt pretty satisfied with my display because Sole was an international player already and I was still trying to break through.

Unfortunately, we lost the final, and once more Wasps had been in front. The front-row contest was satisfying to Wasps and we took a couple of heads when Dawe had to go off after about half an hour. The referee for the second year running was Fred Howard, one of the England international panel. I have always like Fred's style, he is one of the best, principally because he does not go out with any pre-conceived ideas and blows it as he sees it. This time he blew it as he saw it with a couple of penalties against me late in the game for taking the scrum too low and that gave Stuart Barnes a kick to pull Bath up from being 12–4 behind. Bath scored two tries after that and won 19–12 which negated some terrific work by our pack, especially the back row, and by the midfield. That final was never actually played out to its full time because following the second of two pitch invasions, with thousands out from the terraces and stands, the advice to Fred Howard was to end the game, which he did. Much later, probably a couple of years later, I remembered that Jeremy Guscott had played in that final – but only as a wing replacement for Tony Swift.

Chapter Four

NOT WANTED ON VOYAGE

The World Cup came next, played in two countries, Australia and New Zealand, and ended with a recommendation from the organisers that it should be played in future in one country. Everyone knows now that the 1991 Cup was played in five countries so it shows how much notice they took of that recommendation. As England were based in the Australian pool, with Australia, Japan, and the USA, we were to miss out on the action in the co-host country of New Zealand where the Cup, and all the bits and pieces which went with it, were received with much more enthusiasm. Sometimes you would not have known Australia was holding a world-class sporting event in its two principal rugby cities, Sydney and Brisbane. I do not remember a single match being sold out, even when Australia were playing.

There was a semi-glamorous start to the Cup with a launch dinner in Brisbane which we attended with our fellow pool teams. But our home was basically at a hotel in Rushcutter Bay on the south side of Sydney. We trained for a couple of hours each morning, took a couple of hours for lunch, trained again in the afternoon, and took a couple of hours over dinner. That basically was the day, but the nerves tightened as the competition approached with our first match against the co-favourites, Australia. There were just 15 nations in this first Cup – more than 50 were in the race for the 1995 competition – and to kick off the Australian leg it made commercial sense to stage another version of the conflict between Australia and England. That was expected to bring the crowds in and give the tournament a top-grade start, but talking with Australian rugby fans you soon realised that the decision to play the game out of Sydney at a new stadium called the Concord Oval was proving counter-productive. The fans loved the Sydney Cricket Ground because it was in town and close to all of their favourite watering-holes. Concord was not, and the fans voted with their feet for that opening game and fewer than 20,000 were there.

That was a blunder but nothing as serious as that by the New Zealand referee Keith Lawrence who awarded Australia a try which wasn't. David Campese lost contact with the ball going over the line as he chased a kick through but Lawrence was convinced he had scored. It was 6–6 at the time and that 'score' turned the game and Australia headed to a quarter-final against Ireland rather than Wales, our full-back Marcus Rose was on the way home after being put off the pitch with concussion, and what the management saw as the first team had finished a distant second to the Aussies.

I also knew that Pearce had injured his hand and as I could not see any other tight-head props around I reasoned that I would be in for the next game against Japan one week later. There were only three uncapped players in the squad at the start of the Cup – Jon Webb, Dave Egerton and myself. Webb came on for Rose against Australia so Egerton and I thought we might make the next game by which time everyone in the squad would have played. But not so. Pearce had gone so far as to congratulate me on being chosen against Japan, but when the team came out it was like a bolt out of the blue because I was not in it. The management had switched Chilcott over to the tight-head without any explanation. I sought out Martin Green to find out what was happening because I was really hacked off. He said he thought Mike Weston had spoken to me, which was not the case, and said Chilcott had been chosen because he was on the bench and needed a game. He also said that Pearce's hand injury was minor. I pointed out that if we made the semi-finals, for instance, and I had to play I would be without match practice but this drew no response. Weston was not forthcoming either and it became apparent to me that I would not be involved in any team selection by Weston and Green. A lot of the players said I deserved a crack and Chilcott apologised to me. But he had to take the spot and I would have done exactly the same if the situation had been reversed. The bottom line was that I had gone all the way to Australia having been chosen by a management which would not pick me for England unless the front row fell to pieces with injury or illness. I was there for the ride. So, it turned out, was Egerton. So, later, was Micky Skinner who came across as replacement for the injured Jon Hall. It nagged at me, but what could I do?

England coasted to the quarter-finals, beating Japan 60–7 and the Americans 34–6, results which left us second in the qualifying pool behind Australia. Next, the management had planned a mid-tournament break at Hamilton Island off the Queensland coast, and if I was not enjoying what was going on with selection at least this trip provided everyone with a stark contrast to hotel life in Sydney. Even in the Australian winter this was a hot spot and it was just the place, with its warm waters, beaches, and sunshine to change the mood and prepare for the knockout stage of the tournament. There was no thought, when we left that island, that we could possibly lose to Wales on the Ballymore ground in Brisbane.

The events of Cardiff were revived by the media and there was plenty of speculation that there would be more violence between England and Wales which must have worried the management no end because the whole world might be watching this one. The whole business was overplayed, as it often is, but there were enough comments about discipline to make you realise the management wanted everyone to keep the lid on their self-control. There was a significant shift in the forward pattern in that Dooley was moved to the front of the line-out which meant he would not be in direct conflict with Norster, so removing one of the possible flashpoints. The fact that Norster had some kind of injury and limped from line-out to line-out until he went off was not known beforehand. Wales lolled about on the beach the day before the game but Green, against Tom McNab's advice, put us through a three-and-a-half-hour training session in the heat. We were reminded then that England could not afford a repeat of the Cardiff affair and anybody seen throwing a punch would be unlikely to play for England again.

Ironically, the game hinged on another front-row injury, this time to Rendall. He was hurt when a finger went into his eye and he had to come off as we were defending a five-yard scrum. The management did not react quickly enough to the situation and by the time Chilcott had been readied for action England had packed down a man short and suffered the consequences when Gareth Roberts went in for a try for Wales. That was complete embarrassment and the gloom settled over Brisbane in a massive cloud. England were stunned by that score, Wales were lifted, and they added a couple of tries to win 16–3. When you talk about disastrous days, that was one of them. As losers, we were not asked to hang around and watch the rest of the tournament. The inquests began the next morning and there seemed to be plenty of people around the foyer of the hotel prepared to snipe at what they saw as a classic England under-performance. I had to agree with them but I had no wish then or now to moan about not being able to play my full part. It was just another indication that selectors choose teams, not players, and I think selfishly that my only chance of winning a cap would be with someone other than Mike Weston or Martin Green. By the autumn, both Weston and Green had gone from management, victims of the Rugby Union reaction to the World Cup campaign and the under-achievement. There were all kinds of rumours filtering around the game about who would take over. One Friday night, the Rugby Union announced that Geoff Cooke would be the next England manager, initially for one year.

The reaction down south was 'Geoff who?'. I knew he had coached the Northern Division but no more than that. At his first squad sessions, Cooke paid tribute to what had been done in the last couple of years but stressed from the outset that he felt there was much more to come. He saw the English game as one which was conditioned by the fear of failure based on set-piece and kicking rugby. He wanted improvement in fitness, in ball winning and ball retention, and in more effective use of the ball, and an expansion of attitude. From that he believed new confidence would result. The other thing which Cooke did after his appointment was to ask Roger Uttley to be coach. Uttley had been an England captain and a British Lion and had played in the second row and back row and knew the business. He had already coached London and done some line-out work with England so everyone knew him. As a fellow Wasp I knew him better than most.

December was the time for potential England players to show what they could do in the Divisional Championship but in the London side I found myself a loser against the North and the Midlands and we just squeezed by 6–3 against the South-West. But I made the England trial as did the other five front-row men who had been to the World Cup. I made the England side as well in that trial but we were overturned 13–7 so the whole selection process was uncertain. Nobody could say with total confidence that they were in, not with a new management. But when the England team to play France was announced, I was able to hear my name for the first time. Four months short of my 32nd birthday, I had made it.

Playing in Paris will always be special to me because that is where I started off – Parc des Princes, 16 January 1988. I loved everything about going there and for me the match began when we left our hotel at Versailles accompanied by the wailing sirens and flashing blue lights of the police motor-cycle escort all the way to the ground. Those outriders are so skilful and do not think twice about kicking the bodywork of cars they want out of the way. As I was told to sit on the front seat of the coach I had a very good view. But inside I was churning away about the game and here Rendall became very important, telling me what to expect and stressing the pressure and the atmosphere and the need to concentrate. There were two things running through my mind: the joy of achieving a lifetime's ambition and the fear of not being able to perform at that level. I suppose everyone else was feeling the same, especially the other new men, Will Carling and Micky Skinner, but once we were out on the pitch, singing the national anthem, the mere act of doing that was the final bonding of the team.

Much of our history leads us to believe that other nations will dislike us but, unlike the Scots and the Welsh, I have never found that to be the case with the French. You can look at the French players in the tunnel at Parc des Princes and wonder why they have all these bloody nicks on their faces, as if they have been slamming into the walls of the dressing-room, and see the glare in their eyes. But there is no hate there. Brian Moore kept telling me not to give the French anything, 'anything at all, you understand', but you listen to that without taking as much notice as you might. Wade Dooley was behind me, Dean Richards was there, and so was Peter Winterbottom. Why feel concerned with men like that around? And after all, the match was over in ten seconds, or that is how it felt. I still have to look at the videotape to see what happened because the game went so fast that I seem to have missed most of it. I know France objected to England winning a strike against the head because Pascal Ondarts hit me in the face as a result. Moore said that when we won another head there would be a fight. We did, and there was.

The match predictions were that we were going to be stuffed by 30 points but with about a quarter of an hour to go we were ahead 9–3. The England forwards played well that day and Skinner had enjoyed himself, especially with a big tackle on Laurent Rodriguez when he broke from a scrum. Skinner screamed 'Bosch' at the top of his voice, presumably as some sort of stimulant, and halted Rodriguez in his tracks which was a big hit for all of us. But Rodriguez had his revenge, snaffling the try which won the game for France 10–9 after Mike Harrison, our captain, had let a rolling ball slip by. I found Moore in tears at the end, crying in anger and frustration, and gave him a hug as if to say this is the start of something which is going to get better. But we had lost, it was in the book, and the long night which only Paris can provide was to follow.

I was proved wrong in thinking that things would improve when we lost our next game to Wales at Twickenham by 11–3, and already Geoff Cooke was hearing supporters say that the new management team was going to be as bad as the old one and that a whitewash in the Championship was beginning to look a possibility. Wales had punished us for our mistakes, and I had a severe personal lesson in that match because I relaxed against Staff Jones, the Pontypool prop, for just a fraction and he did me the honour of lifting me out of a scrum. I was pretty annoyed because I was feeling comfortable against the Welsh who were more technical than the French but not as physical. The French had attacked me with punches, kicks and a lot of power. I was confident against Wales, perhaps too confident.

I decided to go on one leg and strike for a Welsh put in and the referee, Steve Hilditch of Ireland, asked me to lift the scrum on my side which I did. Staff came in, up I went and I had a pretty good view of Twickenham's West car park. I swear that it is the only time it has happened to me on the international field but it was a bleak few seconds for me. Staff was very generous about it. 'It looks sensational but being popped out is one of those things,' he told me.

So we were two matches down in the Championship and next headed to Scotland with everyone remembering we had conceded 33 points there two years earlier. Harrison went out of the side which gave Oti his first cap and the captaincy went to Melville. We knew we had to play a controlled game to tie the Scots in and if Richards could keep the ball tight it was going to help our cause no end. Sole was now opposite me in an international for the first time but presented no problems. Our control was of the essence and we finished up winners 9–6 though we took a lot of stick from the Scots for what they said were our negative tactics. But we had gone there to win a match by the best means we could and we had turned a corner. That was alright by me. I was a winner in an England shirt at last.

It was a pretty heavy dinner afterwards. I think there was a bottle of Scotch every three or four places at the dining table, plus wine, and most people appeared to be throwing it back like there was no tomorrow. We had all played a hard game and were in the mood to have a good night together, Scots and English. I know that Dooley went to bed early, that Damian Cronin had his face in the soup, and that a food fight had taken place. The speeches were over when someone had the idea that we should go out on the town in Edinburgh and when we set off the Calcutta Cup came with us. The Calcutta Cup is part of rugby folklore because it is fought for annually between England and Scotland, and this precious piece of silverware disappeared into the night and could be seen being passed around the players in the street as if in a seven-a-side tournament. The Cup was taken to a pub called Browns where it was passed around again but on the way back it was used for dropped-goal practice in the street and suffered accordingly. By the time the security men recovered it the damage had been done – and Richards and Scotland's John Jeffrey were subsequently disciplined for their part in the affair. Richards missed one England match and Jeffrey a Scottish tour.

The last game was against Ireland at Twickenham. At half-time we were 3–nil behind and had just seen Melville carried off with obviously severe injuries after being tackled by Tom Clancy. Melville was never to play for England again, which is not something we could judge at that moment, but John Orwin, the second-row forward from Bedford who took over the captaincy, stated that from that moment on we were playing for 'Smellie' Melville as much as anyone else. It was a catalyst for one of the most exciting periods of play in which I have been involved at that level. We decided to run the ball at every opportunity and the tries flowed – three by Oti on his Twickenham debut, two by Rory Underwood and another by Gary Rees from Underwood's running. Here was an England team which had not scored a try in the Championship actually finishing up with half a dozen in one game and the strains of *Swing Low, Sweet Chariot* echoed over Twickenham as never before.

We had an extra game against Ireland for something called the Millennium Trophy, which we won, and I was left to reflect that my first five caps were in the bag. I had found out what international rugby was like; the best experience of all to go into, the worst as well because of the anxiety which goes with the job and whether you are up to it. There are so many watching who can criticise you and wipe you out. I believe I was very fortunate because Uttley knew my capabilities as a player and if there were any questions about my ability he would be able to argue for me. I also felt I had won over selector John Elliott.

After my first international season I was pleased that I could actually cope and still play the game the way I wanted to. You find out whether you have the mental hardness to play at that level because it is more about that than the physical aspect, to be able to make a mistake but still get on with your game. You do not know whether you can cope until you have been there. For example, what happened against Staff Jones had to be followed up in the next scrum by not showing any weakness and re-establishing where I had come from. You learn not to underestimate people and not to overestimate yourself. Everyone you play against is capable of giving you a very nasty shock.

Although we are talking about a team in rugby and working to a team plan with each player dependent on the others, the difference at international level is that you play for yourself within a team framework. When a player is dropped you will never find a great deal of outcry in the team because each player is selfish and jealous regarding their own position. That comes through on the field to a certain extent: if you are out there with a player who is not capable, there will be almost an invisible shunning of him by the others. The game will be played around that player rather than with him as the others perform an act of self-preservation. It happens, not that much, but it happens.

We returned to Australia in May, one year after the World Cup, with a much-changed squad and Orwin as captain. Pearce and I were the tight-head choices but this time I regarded myself as number one at the start of the tour, although I am sure Pearce thought he was as well. If anything, that tour brought us closer together and I think we understood each other better by the end of it.

About half of the World Cup squad made the return trip which meant there were a good many players trying to find their feet within the framework of a tour. Australia were assembling a new team now that Alan Jones, the World Cup coach, had been removed and replaced by Bob Dwyer. England have never won a Test in Australia but we started strongly in the first match in Brisbane and snatched a couple of interception tries through Underwood and John Bentley from Sale who started the tour as a centre and played on the wing in this Test. That left us 13–3 ahead but referee David Bishop started to find so much fault with us that we gave Michael Lynagh enough chances to turn the game. He kicked six penalties which saw Australia through by 22–16.

Simon Halliday who played centre in the first Test went home and Will Carling, who had been taking examinations at Durham

University, flew out to take over and played in the second Test – and against Fiji in Suva when the Aussie section of the tour was over. In between the Tests we took a beating from New South Wales by 23–12 but the same tight five in the pack was retained for the second Test in Sydney with a couple of adjustments in the backs.

The second Test was even more grim. Again we took an early lead with Underwood scoring a try but although the England pack put in a creditable performance we were out of it in the backs where our unsettled and ever-changing line-up could not cope against the more assured and faster Australian play. They ran in four tries to our two and won 28–8. Cooke was caustic about the state of our game when he looked at the Australian section of the tour which had taught us that we had to change our style and attitude. The Australians had told him they saw England as a side which went from one set piece to another, trying to gain penalties. Cooke, like the rest of us, knew we would play Australia again at Twickenham the following autumn. The message was there – we had to improve.

We finished the tour by beating Fiji. I have been to the Fiji islands a couple of times now and at first glance it seems surprising that they actually play such good rugby there, given the climate and the lifestyle. It is always hot and humid and the pitches either resemble dust bowls or are awash after one of those tropical downpours. The word now is that Fiji have slackened off a little as a 15-a-side team and need to regroup, but we were expecting no favours that day in a match where Pearce was selected at tight-head. We decided to stop the Fijians shooting all over the park by driving into their pack in numbers and forcing them to stay in contact. The Fijians did not like it but had to knuckle down and spent the game in frustration as we maintained the pressure. They could counter-attack well but we kept grinding away, making two tries for Underwood and another for Bryan Barley, and won 25–12. Almost the last act of the game was a savage punch on Gary Rees from one of the frustrated Fijian forwards. Rees went down and then off with a cut lip, and Egerton just beat the final whistle from Kerry Fitzgerald, the Aussie referee, and ran on as replacement.

The tour was over. No one could claim we had progressed as a side. But Cooke had now had eight Tests under his control – won four, lost four, and as we began our journey home who would have guessed what Cooke was going to do next?

I don't think anyone anticipated what Cooke would do with the captaincy – but I suspected correctly he would not continue with Alan Davies and David Robinson who came on the Australian tour as part of the management/coaching team. I had enjoyed working under Davies in the B game in 1987 and was ready for his relaxed approach on the tour – he and Robinson were new boys to the touring scene at this level and were there because Uttley could not travel. Davies liked everyone to settle down over dinner, have a bottle of wine, break into groups to discuss about 30 questions he had posed, and then come up with the answers. Davies went to Australia with the belief that he was the England coach, or at least the coach-in-waiting.

Orwin, the tour captain, underwent a personality change once he had the leadership and people who knew him well said he was completely different during that trip. For example, we had a system of fines if people were late for appointments and he was insistent that they were paid. One day he was late for the bus, caught it up down the road, and refused to pay his fine which threw the whole thing into disarray. He seldom trained a full session and only kept his place because he was captain. It was against this background that the tour started in a sugar town called Mackay in Queensland with Davies in command on the pitch. Robinson, a farmer from Cumbria, had brought his shepherd's crook along and used to hold it out at the height he considered the maximum for forwards going into rucks and this was one of his methods of getting us into the right frame of mind.

Davies ran the backs session which brought him into direct conflict with Cooke who also considered himself a backs coach. We had an unbalanced backline anyway and by the time we approached the end of the tour Cooke had taken over and Davies virtually held up his hands in submission. Just before the second Test, when we were in Adelaide, Davies seemed resigned to the fact he had no future with that England set-up and although he continued to try to bring the best out of the boys you could tell his heart was not in it. We stopped discussing the way the game should be played and were given a way to play the game instead. Cooke is a much more analytical person and can sit and watch videos and work on things before deciding on the way he expects a game to be played. He also tends to pick people who are fairly malleable to his way of thinking.

Orwin was unfit for that last game in Fiji and Richard Harding was made captain. But he had reached the magic age of 36, the pencil came out, and no more was he seen in the England squad.

Chapter Five

AUSTRALIA TAMED

The next thing which was emphasised to the players in the England squad, and by this time I mean the top 60 or so players in the country, was the need for improved fitness. No one could escape because fitness testing was to be carried out at regular intervals and progress, or lack of it, would become obvious from the charts and statistics. The toughest thing of all was called the bleep test, and I know of players who approach this with a degree of apprehension because it is so revealing. It is a simple test in which you run over a 20-metres course at differing speeds, always moving up a notch in pace, against a bleep coming from a tape recorder. There are at least 20 levels but I think the best anyone has done is just over 14, achieved by Ian Hunter who is one of the most phenomenal trainers I have ever known. I have been satisfied with most of my performances against the bleep – and been warned if I fell behind. I have a two-edged view on testing because I realise its value, but also believe that Seb Coe would do well on the bleep test but would not be able to last one scrum or one line-out in the sort of company I keep on the rugby pitch.

England players from just a few years ago tell me there is no way they would be able to live with the present team in terms of fitness and I would have to agree with them because I know what has happened to my own performance. We come under scrutiny from Rex Hazeldine of Loughborough University who advises England on fitness, and he tells me that as the oldest player in the squad at the start of 1993 my speed times were quite exceptional. He puts us through a routine of 15- and 30-metre sprints, standing jumps, press-ups, sit-ups and a strength test, and the detailed analysis of these shows exactly where you are going. Rory Underwood began the year once more as England's fastest player over the two sprint distances and Mike Teague was the quickest forward at 15 metres. Rob Andrew came out as the best all-rounder in the backs and Peter Winterbottom entered his last season in international rugby with great endurance, leg power and speed readings. We also have to test for body-fat content, changes in which indicate a player's success in replacing excess fat with muscle.

I have never been certain that the fitness aspect is as important as has been claimed, because if you are in an international side you have reached a high degree of fitness on your own. But the fact that you have to attain a set of figures concentrates the mind and you consciously look to get fitter whether you follow the programmes religiously or not. Any player who has a full working day would just not have the spare time to fit in the extra training load. It is not just finding an hour a day to work out, it is the getting there, the getting back, which takes the time. To prepare for the testing I started to put in some road running, which I never used to do, and Rendall encouraged me to go with him after the normal Wasps session. We would put in a two-mile timed run, sometimes four miles, in the early part of the season. I still believe that they should test everyone's lung capacity first and use that as a basis for what comes next. In that way I think they will find the right type of make-up for rugby.

As for the bleep test, I think you can fool it. When I was tested for the first time and recorded 10.7 it was suggested to me that I put in extra training. I pointed out that my daily routine was to be up at 6.00 a.m., in my business an hour later, work through until 6.00 p.m. and be free by about 9.00 p.m. Where was I to find the time for extra training on top of the two club sessions I did already? I was then asked – what about Sunday? Which was a bit of a joke because I did like one day off from rugby. The best thing for the bleep test is to record a low score at first and then come on with a dramatic improvement in mid-season which makes you look better than many who start high and cannot go up much more. My scores over the last few years have reflected my approach.

Everyone I have played against is at least a stone heavier than I am, so I do not want to drop off any more weight. Sole was one of the lightest, others are over 17 stone. Of course I have to be fit to play against those sort of weights but it is just as important to me to be sure of my muscle tone, general strength, and sharpness in scrummaging technique as it is to satisfy the test figures. I have also done hours of training on my own – living where I do it's tough enough getting someone to come over for a drink, let alone train.

Everyone has changed diet and eats to a much more controlled regime these days with pasta, fish and chicken at the top of the list, and Geoff Cooke has been fairly firm in requesting that players stay away from alcohol for the three days before a match. Most do out of habit anyway – the way rugby is going at the top it will lose its beer-swilling image well before the end of the century – and others are learning. But I know lots of players for whom a Friday night stroll and a pint is the best way of calming the nerves before a major game. I also know that testing will become even more severe. The idea is for the England players to be improving by up to 15 per cent on the various tests in time for the 1995 World Cup and I am sure that will be achieved. Rex has another scheme up his sleeve called Creeping Paralysis which shows how much endurance a player has for a game in which there might be more than 120 different sequences of play. It is easy to appreciate now why players never actually slacken off training – they just keep aiming for a series of peaks laid down by the management in relation to fixtures.

I had come back from Australia with a residue of fitness and kept myself in trim for the start of the 1988–89 season. My first priority was to make the London side against Australia and the first step towards that was a warm-up game against Munster in Cork. Paul Ackford played in the second row for London only a few months after appearing for Harlequins in their Cup final win over Bristol at Twickenham. He was then 30, and considering he played for England B all the way back in 1979 he was basically unfulfilled. He had been in the London team against the 1984 Australians and thanks to some carefully calculated nagging by Dick Best, then the Harlequins coach, he had been giving rugby at a higher level yet another shot. London did not choose Ackford as an original selection to go to Munster but he filled in for Sean O'Leary who was abroad. Ackford took this game as the only one he was ever going to play at that level again and he was magnificent. We had a good night in Cork and kept the mood going at breakfast where we ordered champagne and kept sending the corks over to the London treasurer, Alan Parker, so that he could see what was happening. The treasurer insisted he was not paying but Ackford produced £10, told the waiter to bring two more bottles, and when he had done so suggested he went to the treasurer for the extra. Ackers, I feel sure, was ready to bow out in style.

Back in London, Ackford and I jumped on the Underground train from Heathrow and we began talking about the relative merits of the second-row forwards who were around at the time pushing for international selection. London had Neil Edwards, who had decided to play for Scotland, and it was a question of whether O'Leary would be back to play with him. I said that based on the game Ackford had played against Munster the selectors would have to play him against Australia, and I would have played O'Leary with him. Now Ackford did win the vote against Australia and he played a very relaxed game based on the fact that he did not think he was going any higher. The switching of his role to the front of the line-out was something which was totally new to him and we did a lot of work together to develop his jumping there.

London were first up against Nick Farr-Jones and his Australians. Cooke had overseen a debate involving the four chairmen of selectors and coaches of the four divisions who were to play the Australians, and there was a general agreement that the game had to be taken to them and that the individual teams would work on their own refinements. Best, coach to London, had seven of his Harlequins in the team and the pace was set and the challenge tossed down to the other divisions when London won 21–10. It had been a good, well-crafted performance by London and it was gratifying to see that mood maintained throughout the country. The North beat them 15–9 at Otley and a scrum-half named Dewi Morris scored a try for the North in that game to mark his first appearance on that stage. Next the South-West dumped the Australians 26–10 at Bristol and the final divisional game just turned against a clean sweep when the Midlands were beaten 25–18.

England now had to do even better than the three victorious divisions and Cooke named a team which reflected the form, with Ackford chosen for his debut along with Morris at half-back and the London wing Andy Harriman, the Nigerian scoring king. The captain was Carling who was the youngest player in the team at 22 and the youngest player to captain England for 57 years. It did not end there – Cooke had pencilled in Carling to take England all the way to the 1991 World Cup. So this was Cooke's answer for the future. England had played under four captains in 1988, Harrison, Melville, Orwin and Richard Harding in Fiji, and Carling was to become the fifth, with the offer of a long-term place. Carling called heads or tails beforehand – and let the rest of us get on with the game.

Because of the divisional results we were quite confident and this was reflected completely in our 28–19 win which left the Australians whingeing that it was the early part of their tour and they were not yet at the top of their game. They paid us no compliments but the damage was there for all to see on the pitch. Ackford, as I had expected, performed superbly at the front of the line-out and was no longer a neglected and unmotivated force. He was there to stay, not only for his own skills but because he eased the burden on Dooley and so made life easier for him. It was not a one-way victory because Australia were in front twice and we were down 13–9 before we actually took a real grip on the game. Rory Underwood scored twice in quick succession to change the game and late on Carling sent Halliday away for our fourth try to put the result beyond any doubt. Carling missed the last few minutes because he had concussion but he would have sensed the mood of elation in the dressing-room. For those who had had to endure three losing Tests in a row to the Aussies, and especially for Rory who had lost four times running, it was a sweet day.

London won the Divisional Championship the following month with a vastly superior points difference over the North and Cooke took the England squad to Portugal a month ahead of the 1989 Championship where Carling developed the first of the leg problems which were with him for the first half of the year and forced him to miss our game in Romania and then the British Lions tour of Australia – for which everyone in the squad was shooting. With Ian McGeechan of Scotland appointed Lions coach and Roger Uttley as his deputy it was also obvious that many of the selection questions could be answered in the England–Scotland game which opened the Championship. The Calcutta Cup, fully restored after the events of 1988, was also available for competition.

Scotland came to Twickenham with the sole aim of trying to frustrate any attempt by England to play with the ball and return the game to the chaotic style they benefit from. McGeechan would have looked at the way we played against Australia and devised a plan to counter that which basically meant making the game a very stop-start affair. There was a lot of tension around on both sides, too many unforced errors, too many old scores being revived, and the whole match was mostly a misery. The 12–12 result benefited nobody, but the Scots probably felt better about it than we did.

There was only one try in the match and as that was scored by Jeffrey it made up for his problems over the Calcutta Cup the previous year. Craig Chalmers put up a high ball which Jon Webb dropped under pressure and in came Jeffrey to kick through and follow up for the touchdown. We were 12–6 down before two penalties by Webb brought us level, but between them Webb and Andrew put wide seven kicks at goal. It was just nobody's day and the elation we felt after beating Australia was a distant memory. We were meant to be Championship favourites but that result showed how off-beam that prediction was. And little did I realise that my international season, indeed my international year, was about to suffer a serious set-back.

In the next match against Ireland in Dublin I came off having been judged to be suffering from concussion. To this day I am not certain what happened but having looked at the video a few times I know that I dived on a ball after a line-out. At the same time, Jim McCoy, the Irish prop, must have decided that he wanted to kick the ball into the crowd and instead he kicked my head. I remained on the field for about 20 minutes but have no memory of that time and was obviously in a fairly bad way. Half-time came and went without my knowledge and Brian Moore insisted to the referee, Les Peard of Wales, that our trainer Kevin Murphy take a look at me and I was taken off the field. When I came off I was just about coming back to my senses and I might have been able to carry on. But I know it was for the best that I came off – and Gareth Chilcott took over – and I also knew that I would not be allowed to play for three weeks because I had sustained concussion. That put the French match out of the window – and the other prizes which were available that spring in doubt.

I went from player to spectator and did not enjoy the experience. I was pleased that England continued to go forward and followed up the 16–3 win in Ireland with an 11–nil win over France at Twickenham. This was England, disciplined and powerful, giving the defending champions a roasting. We had gone ten years without a home win over the French and France had gone 36 years without ending a game at Twickenham with no points. Having been so involved I did not like being a spectator. I was a guest for the day and felt the lack of involvement and preparations for the game greatly. It is something I will remember for a long time and it taught me that the best way to watch is on television.

I had hoped to make it back for the last game against Wales. I resumed playing with Wasps and felt in good shape physically. But the selectors kept the side which had beaten France, understandably from their point of view I suppose, but no explanation was given to me. Chilcott continued at prop in Cardiff which put him up against Mike Griffiths. Griffiths put sufficient pressure on Chilcott to disrupt the England scrum and we spent too much time in our own half. From my seat on the bench I could see that Griffiths was playing well and indeed he took himself into the Lions side on that performance.

England's opportunity to end the misery of not winning at Cardiff was short lived. It was a wet and miserable day and Mike Teague was taken out of the game when Wales kicked off. He suffered concussion, just as I did, and knew little of what went on that afternoon. Teague's support play was critical to the line-out and without it we were not the same force, and Norster, with his athletic leaping and two-handed secure catching, had a field day. In the rain Robert Jones box-kicked to perfection and between them these two players inflicted a fair amount of territorial damage. It was still a close match but as Wales won two-thirds of the ball they deserved to win. The try which decided it, the only one of the game, followed a rare England incursion into the Welsh half. Wales cleared the ball deep into our half and Underwood picked it up and, without looking, switched it back towards Webb. That left Wales with a gift ball to kick on and Mike Hall followed through and was given the touchdown. It finished 12–9 and I started to wonder if I was going to create another kind of record by sitting on the bench in Cardiff while England failed to win. Two visits, two defeats. It was not looking so good. Already I was fed up with the bench and when the Lions party to go to Australia was announced and I was not in it I felt like telling England they could stick their place on the bench somewhere where the sun does not shine.

Chapter Six

TRYING IN BUCHAREST

The spring of 1989 found me far from happy. I had been put out of the England side by injury, lost my place to Gareth Chilcott, and when the Lions chose the squad to tour Australia I was not in that either. Chilcott was. This meant I had suffered disappointment on two fronts only a year after getting into the England side. Despondent was hardly the word for it.

In the close season England had arranged to play Romania in Bucharest and when I was chosen for the match squad, but not the team, it did nothing for my depression, and the more I thought about it, the more I considered making a grand gesture by doing something like pulling out. This appealed to me greatly because I felt I had been messed around a fair amount and Geoff Cooke's style of not talking to people who were out of the side had left me with no explanation. Sure, Chilcott had come in because I was injured in Ireland. But once I was cleared to play again I believed I should have returned to the team.

I made sure that a few close friends knew that I was hacked off with the situation and that I was really set on pulling out, even though

I knew that it might have been the end of any serious involvement with that or any subsequent England squad. The few close friends did the trick because they kept hammering at me to swallow my pride and keep going. Roger Uttley heard of my mood and telephoned me. He said that he could not tell me what had gone on in selection but urged me not to drop out. I got the message.

It was a long day down to Romania, into Zurich and out again on another flight, and very few of us had a clue about what we would find when we arrived there. Romania was still a few months away from the assassination of President Nicolai Ceaucescu and out of all the places I had been to on the rugby circuit this was certainly a very different regime. But it did not detract from the fact that Romania had a respected side, greatly influenced by regular contact with France. At one time Romania had improved so much that there was talk of them coming into the Five Nations Championship. But nothing happened.

Going into Bucharest seemed like a step back into history once you were in the centre of the city and beyond the blocks of flats which seemed to cover miles on the way from the airport. We stayed in an old hotel, dimly lit, the foyer full of people who seemed to be smoking heavily and wanting to do black-market currency deals. If you had a few US dollars you felt as if you could buy the moon.

The Rugby Union, true to form, had done their homework. We took all of our food and drink requirements with us – well, not draught beer because that was available on tap in the hotel, providing you paid in foreign currency – and we were so well provisioned that we were able to leave some behind. You had only to look at the food which our supporters were offered in the hotel restaurant to realise that the Rugby Union were right.

Preparing for the match was no different to anywhere else. There was an international to be played and we trained as normal. I knew I was going to be on the bench at the August 23 stadium but still had to pay attention to all the detail of the forward play. There were three players making their first appearances for England – Simon Hodgkinson at full-back, who might have come in a year earlier but for a bad trial, Jeremy Guscott at centre, and my fellow Wasp Steve Bates at scrum-half. Guscott had a huge reputation even then and had come in because Will

Carling was injured, an arrangement which continued on the Lions tour. Rob Andrew was captain, for the first time.

England took an under-21 side to Romania as well. A prop named Jason Leonard was playing in that side and, having heard a little about him, I took a close look. The under-21 side was so on top that Jason was never under pressure – little could he have realised that he was only 15 months away from his senior debut.

Romania sounded like difficult opponents. Only five months before they had beaten Wales in Cardiff, which is something England had been unable to do in that same season, and there was every reason to believe that they were going to be a handful.

Two little incidents involving Coca-Cola stay in my mind from Bucharest. At a reception of the British Embassy the night before the match we had been given some cans of Coke to take back to our hotel, Coke not being readily available at the time. We left a couple of cans on the table in the hotel and one of the waiters, clearly nervous, asked if he might have one. It turned out that the waiter wanted one for his child's birthday so we gave him all that was left, about half a dozen cans in all. Another waiter who had watched and listened to the entire affair burst into tears, overcome by the fact that we had given away what to him was an unobtainable product.

When the Romania–England match kicked off I had a can of Coke in my hand. It was about 90 degrees that afternoon and I was thirsty as I sat there, with my boots untied, under a canopy watching the game get going. Then Chilcott tore a calf muscle, John Olver screamed at me to say I should get on the pitch fast, and I threw the can away and went on to the pitch, laces flapping.

After all the build-up, Romania proved to be disappointing opponents. The England pack played particularly well in the heat and we gave them little room to move. As a result we had plenty of opportunities and the backs took them well. Guscott had a sensational debut with a hat trick of tries and Chris Oti on the wing scored four as England won 58–3. I am proud to say that I scored my first try for England in that game. Brian Moore took a quick throw at a line-out 25 yards out and I just ran through and dived in for a score. Very satisfying.

There was a lot to praise in the England performance. Hodgkinson reminded everyone of his place-kicking skills with eight conversions and a penalty, and Andrew and Bates had enjoyed themselves at half-back, so much so that it is surprising that Bates has not won another cap. But the revelation was Guscott. Outside of the Bath lads, few of us knew him but every stride he took that day, each change of pace or direction, and everything he did with the ball marked him down as class.

I was just pleased to play again after all the disappointments of the previous few weeks. I came off the Coca-Cola and on to the beer to celebrate. There were Romanian wines at the after-match banquet. With a live band and traditional dancing it was quite a night. Only outside, in the near deserted streets, did you realise that Romania was a country in the grip of an oppressive dictator. Just strolling around at night the few people you saw were involved in security. It was a strange feeling to be part of that atmosphere, even for our short stay.

On the way home I resigned myself to a summer of inactivity. Until the tour to South Africa came out of the blue I was right. The word was that Chilcott would recover from his calf injury and go on the Lions tour. Only if he or one of the other props withdrew before the tour or was injured during it would I stand a chance of being a Lion. No chance came, the Lions won the series against Australia 2–1, and soon another season was beckoning. Unbeknown to me, the Lions were to play again after the Australian tour – and I was to wear the shirt after all.

The four home unions had been asked to send a team to Paris to play France in a floodlit match at Parc des Princes to mark part of rugby's contribution to the bicentenary of the French republic. This meant that the Lions could play again but some of the players who had been in Australia objected to being involved in this one-off game unless they could take their wives or girlfriends with them.

So it was not quite a representative Lions side which went to Paris under Rob Andrew's captaincy. All the backs had been on the tour but in the pack Damian Cronin of Scotland, Dave Egerton of England, and Phil Matthews of Ireland joined me as non-Lions. But after the game, which we won 29–27, coach Ian McGeechan declared that he was proud of the Lions. I held on to my Lions shirt as a memento of that evening, hoping that I would be able to add more in 1993. It was not to be.

The rest of the autumn of 1989 was not uplifting. I had heard that Will Carling considered myself and Paul Rendall were too old for England and had said so to Steve Bates when Bates was considering whether to go to South Africa. Maybe Will was a bit put out because the South Africans did not invite him. The autumn match that season was against Fiji and at a meeting earlier the players kicked around the subject of who they thought the centres should be without anyone actually coming forward and saying their piece. The stalemate was broken by Rendall who said he thought Simon Halliday and Guscott, the pairing against Romania, should continue. That would have left Carling out and the matter was not pursued, but at another meeting Carling said that the forwards had been too slow around the pitch against Wales the previous March and it then became obvious to me that Rendall and myself would not be chosen against Fiji.

But England did not let me go completely. I was put into the B team with Kevin Dunn of Gloucester and Jason Leonard as my front-row colleagues to play Fiji at Headingley. I was not surprised to see Leonard there but I was surprised when we lost the game 20–12 which was not a good omen for anyone in that B team.

I went to Twickenham a few days later as a spectator. Rendall was on the bench, I was out, and the props were Andy Mullins and Mark Linnett in a pack which was pretty much the number-one line-up. It was a heavy-scoring game with Rory Underwood scoring five out of 14 tries in a 58–23 win. The Fijians had a couple of players, both backs, sent off and really it was not much of a contest. Nothing happened in that game to suggest that Rendall and myself were out of the front row for good.

Chapter Seven

THE ALTERNATIVE TOUR

I kept a close eye on the Lions while they were in Australia. When the Irish fly-half Paul Dean was injured in the very first game against Western Australia and had to come home it was a rapid indication of how the best-laid plans of a touring team can be upset. When Rob Andrew flew out to replace him who could have predicted that he would come from the standby reserves to play in the second and third Tests, which the Lions won? But when Dean came back, all those who thought they had a chance of going out as a reserve, myself included, were given a little hope. In my case, nothing materialised.

Even though I was not in Australia, one of the off-field things which happened there filtered back through the grapevine. At the end of that summer the South African Rugby Board was staging its centenary celebrations and wanted an international squad to go there on tour and play a few games. I know that the Lions were asked if they would go and that the players met and decided that they would travel to South Africa as long as they were well rewarded. The Lions balanced the fact that they would not mind an additional tour that year against the flak which would fly in their direction for going. At that time South Africa had not been accepted back on to the world stage. That had to wait until 1992. I heard that the Lions thought that £100,000 a man would be a proper figure for taking part in a tour. Whether that was true or not only those parties closely involved would know. But the Lions did not travel to South Africa.

This did not prevent the South Africans pressing on with the tour they so wanted for their players and spectators who had been deprived of regular international contact. The South Africans started to use their contacts in Europe and I had a couple of phone calls which suggested to me they were trying to arrange a squad of England players to go there. That fell through as well, and the next thing I heard was that there were two South Africans moving around Britain trying to recruit players. Apparently these two tried to contact Brian Moore but he was not prepared to talk to them. The South Africans persisted in their hunt for an English contact and were given the name of Paul Rendall. Rendall let me know that the South Africans were interested in my going there and subsequently I went to meet the two gentlemen in the Cavendish Hotel in central London. I said the only way I would consider going was if the invitation was made through official channels. In other words, they had to ask the Rugby Union at Twickenham for my services. I wanted it done no other way.

Two days later, the Rugby Union said that they had had this invitation from South Africa for me. They had also inquired about Paul Rendall, Peter Winterbottom and Mike Teague. We had three days to make up our minds and I was influenced by Dudley Wood, the secretary at Twickenham, who said that the tour of South Africa by an international squad had been sanctioned by the Rugby Union. I decided that I would go.

The English were not alone in being wanted. A contingent of Welsh players was being put together by Bob Norster and Paul Thorburn, Steve Smith, the Irish hooker, accepted to travel, and the wing Keith Robertson became the only Scot to go. France and Australia were also to provide players and the squad was to be managed by Willie John McBride, the Irishman who was a former Lions captain and manager, and coached by Bob Templeton of Australia who had then been involved with the top end of rugby for approaching 20 years.

We had a meeting to discuss the tour in more detail and halfway through John Kendall-Carpenter, a former England captain and past president of the Rugby Union and at the time the chairman of Rugby World Cup, entered the room to say how much he appreciated what we were doing for rugby by going to South Africa and how much he understood the pressures which were to be faced by ourselves and our families as a result. But he assured us that by going to South Africa we were in effect saving the amateur game. If we did not go he believed that the South Africans would have established a professional circus to ensure that they had a tour. And he emphasised that our venture had the full sanction of the leading nations. I took his warning about families being under pressure seriously. I bought an answerphone so my family could screen all calls. We were not bothered, but others were.

Four of us formed an advance party from London – Willie John McBride, Steve Smith, Paul Rendall and myself. Smith travelled in a track suit and when we arrived at Jan Smuts airport in Johannesburg he was spotted immediately by the crowds in the arrival hall and almost swamped. There must have been a crowd of 200 around him. Rendall and I, wearing suits, were completely unnoticed by the fans and walked unheeded to a coffee shop where we watched the whole business.

It was difficult to believe we were actually there. South Africa always has to be a target in the mind of any rugby player but the opportunities to go were so restricted. There had been an England tour there in 1984, for which I did not come close to being selected, but I had heard from the lads who went on that trip how wide the gap had been between them and the South African players.

Of course I was aware of the political situation in South Africa and that apartheid was still being dismantled. Any rugby player of my generation had grown up with the realisation that South Africa was slowly becoming more and more off-limits and that a country which had been used to hosting tours from all the top countries had gradually been almost cut off. I had this vision of the blacks in South Africa being totally oppressed but in my extremely short time there – the first match on the First National Bank World XV tour was on 19 August and the last on 1 September – I realised that I was wrong. From what I saw at the time, there was a fair degree of harmony in a society which is impossible to comprehend unless you actually go there.

The three players who were first in Johannesburg, Smith, Rendall, and myself, decided to put the journey out of our system by going for a run at Ellis Park, the main Test ground in South Africa. Each of us knew we were having our first run at altitude but had no idea of the effect it would have upon us. At the end of our first length of the field I felt as though someone had cut a hole in the back of my throat. Whatever we did in that thinner atmosphere was hard and tiring. I realised straightaway that the climatic conditions alone would make this a difficult trip.

In our luxury hotel that night we began to feel more at home. For a start one of the bars was called Judge's Bar, which pleased Rendall (whose nickname is the Judge) no end, and after we had tried the local lager and some kind of stout brewed in Nairobi which tasted like liquorice water we hit on the front-row drink for the tour, Daiquiris. The three of us had quite a night on this drink and insist that we maintain that tradition on the rare occasions that we now meet.

You would not have thought that three front-row forwards would need special protection. But the South African Rugby Board did. Three security men, all obviously armed, were assigned to watch over us and kept their distance while we continued on our settling-in process. Eventually we asked them to join us in a drink or two and by midnight they had to call in for replacements because the first wave were in need of a little protection for themselves. We became a popular shift for the guards who clearly saw us as political targets for any one of a number of groups and that was why they had to be there. They seemed like the equivalent of what I imagine the SAS to be and when they told us that Nelson Mandela would be released within the next few months it was some proof that they knew what was going on in their country.

Gradually the tour party grew until it was 30 strong. McBride busied himself with building team spirit as quickly as possible because he saw that as a vital factor if we were to have any serious chance against South Africa in the two Tests to be played in Cape Town and Johannesburg.

I awaited the arrival of the French players with interest. I knew some of them from the couple of matches I had played for England against France but beyond that had no real association. We had not mixed much and communication either way is not that straightforward. When they turned up in South Africa they had mislaid their boots – so trained barefoot. They put on a magical display and Greg Martin, the Australian full-back was impressed. 'Look at them,' he said. 'If they can run like that without boots what will they be like when they get them?'

Pierre Berbizier, the French captain and later the national coach, was given the captaincy of the tour squad. That was a good move because he could run the French players and spoke sufficient English to keep everyone else informed and interested. He could play a bit, as well. Pierre also came up with cases of wine for our meeting before the first match against Natal and if there were any lingering doubts about the tour squad gelling they were put to rest that night. The wine helped smooth over any difficulties in communication.

The first game cost us Keith Robertson who had his knee stamped on quite viciously and hurt his ligaments. We played five games in all and I took part in three. I had one Test, the first, which we lost 20–19, in Cape Town. It meant that I did not play at altitude but after my experience on the first day I did not object to that. The second Test also went to South Africa 22–16 and as a scratch squad we had good reason to feel satisfied.

As I have said, this tour was officially sanctioned and the South African Rugby Board paid me the official daily allowance of £20. I presume everyone else received the same. Outside of that, I was asked to speak at a number of functions and make public appearances at events. For these activities, which were not rugby related, I received payment. These payments compensated me to a degree for the loss of earnings while I was abroad and were subject to income tax in South Africa, which I paid. The Inland Revenue in this country knows because they investigated the circumstances of the tour later.

The structure of payments in South Africa is much the same as that which is allowable now. We were possibly slightly ahead of the game but we were allowed to receive money as a group of players for functions we attended, and I did so because a business like mine does not carry any dead weight and being in South Africa did nothing for my business back home. People had the illusion that players on that tour came home with great wedges of money. I can speak only for myself when I say that four years on I still have the same car and same house. My life certainly did not change as a result of going to South Africa. The bonus I did get was some new friends in the game. And you cannot measure really knowing someone like Phillippe Sella of France on a balance sheet.

South Africa still had three years to go before being accepted back into international rugby. Near isolation had affected them. The players certainly were not on a par with the oustanding South African sides of the past. The South African players I saw needed exposure to other countries, other ideas, and then they would stand a chance of catching up.

There could have been few people in the world of rugby who did not want that visit to South Africa to take place. I am convinced all the authorities wanted it and when presentations were made to Dr Danie Craven, president of the South African Rugby Board, after the second and final Test, all the major countries except England were involved in the high-profile ceremony. For some reason, the presentation from the Rugby Football Union was made in a different part of the room, away from the glare of the lights and cameras but in front of the small group of England players who were present.

Chapter Eight

GRAND SLUMP

I believed 1990 was going to be our year. You could feel that the various units in the side were gelling better, understanding one another more, and if you looked back at 1989 we should have beaten Scotland and not let the Welsh match slip. Surely this time we had the belief and the resources to do it. That was the theme of the pre-Championship training camp – the first – in Lanzarote and I, for one, had gone there confident after playing for London in the divisional competition and winning all three matches.

Carling heightened his profile in the run-in to the first game against Ireland which had followed the usual lines of Wednesday evening assembly with the normal training sessions and team meetings to follow. But on the Thursday afternoon, normally free time for the squad, Will announced that he was calling another meeting, something which had not happened before in my experience. When we entered the River Room at the Petersham Hotel we were confronted by TV lights and cameras and Will came in to give us this big speech on motivation. He stressed that we should let Ireland know they were beaten men, which I actually believed was true without him telling me. The last thing I needed at that point was motivation and I felt that direction would have been more appropriate. If you were not switched on for that game you did not deserve to be there. The whole business did not take too long and of course at the end of the season we discovered why – the talk was part of a video on England, with Carling as one of the stars.

I thought we might take Ireland to the cleaners and the record book says we won 23–nil. In fact, we struggled to take control for an hour and only truly dominated Willie Anderson's men in the last quarter. From a personal point of view it was a very satisfying experience because I scored a try. Ireland had been giving us the usual degree of hassle but made little of their possession. Even so, we were stumbling along as a team and it was from a break by Underwood that I scored. Rory was checked around the Irish 22 but put a pass inside which missed Skinner and I took the ball from fairly close range and was over. All that was overtaken by the scores which came later in the game and Rory pushed himself into the position of all-time highest try-scorer for England with his 19th touchdown.

Everyone accepted that our performance against Ireland was a long way short of our targets and that we needed a much tighter display to follow in France or the campaign would founder very quickly. Our practice was good and the bits and pieces we needed to do on the Friday went smoothly. But we woke on the Saturday morning to find Paris being battered by howling gales thundering in from the east. As we sorted ourselves out in the dressing-room the word filtered through that the B team had drawn 15–15 with France. What we did not know was that the winds had blown away a couple of marquees at the end of the ground which was next door to Parc des Princes. We took our customary look around the ground and the wind showed no sign of slackening and ripped into our faces. Obviously it was going to be difficult for the kickers with paper and rubbish being blown all over the place. Hoardings were tumbling down.

For my second visit to Paris I received the customary welcome for an England prop from Ondarts. I looked at the ball as it came into the first line-out and got a big smack on the jaw from Ondarts. If

France feel you are a threat to them or their team they will try and take you out. Your opposite number will hit you and if that does nothing they put two guys on you to throw you off the game. If that fails they back off and try someone else to see if they can break up the patterns of your play. If they don't hit you, it means you are not troubling them. You have to live through the hitting but as a relative new boy I was still getting the smacks. We won 26–7, which was a bigger score than we deserved, but the bounces fell for us and Simon Hodgkinson had a fabulous day with his goal kicking and gave us a platform of three penalties early in the game. When it was within his range he took the kick and you could see France going down at the same time. They dreaded him because they knew he would punish them. What a contrast for Simon to his 1988 trial at Twickenham when, in similar conditions, he had had a howler. This time he struck four penalties and a conversion on a day he should savour for evermore. We had three good tries from the backs – Underwood, Guscott, and finally Carling – and once more I felt that Paris was my kind of town. And as usual after a win over France we were thrust into the position of favourites to take Wales, fully justified as it turned out.

I wanted to get at Wales because I had missed the 1989 match and because it would be my first game against Griffiths. I was told he had been the best scrummager in the 1989 Lions and that fact alone keyed me up more than usual. I saw it as a very big challenge and the rest of the pack caught my mood. The first scrum on the Welsh put in was the best scrum I have ever been in for England. We pushed them back five yards and right off the ball, and that really set the seal on the game and which way it was going. I doubted the Welsh heart for the battle that day and there were enough wheezing noises to doubt their fitness as well. It turned out that Griffiths was carrying a bit of an injury and with so many virtually turning it in up front, bar the great play of Phil Davies, I almost began to feel sorry for Wales. Almost – our 34–6 win said it all because it was a record in all ways. John Ryan, the Welsh coach, was only to survive a couple more days. Robert Jones was shell-shocked. 'How are we going to live this down at home,' he asked me. Around me in the Hilton Hotel in London that evening, as the night flowed on, I heard talk of nothing but a Grand Slam for

England now. We had pulled off a fantastic win which had made us proud and made Twickenham throb, but Scotland had to be beaten at Murrayfield, a month away, for the Slam to become a reality.

The confidence for going to Murrayfield was felt more in the backs than the forwards. The forwards understood that in every game you play, even when you win by a lot of points, there is always confrontation, always something physical. It is always easier when the backs are running in tries because you are going forward more often and the opposition have to turn. Even when we won easily against Ireland that year, for instance, I came out damaged with my left earlobe almost ripped off after Des Fitzgerald, the Irish prop, did a little tap-dance on my head. I played on with the ear bandaged and had to have 15 stitches put in it afterwards. It looks like a patchwork quilt these days, a little reminder that if something comes your way you accept it. If you whinge, you should not be playing. Ireland are not overtly dirty, just very physical, and you have to meet them as a collective force.

Each country has its own characteristics. France are macho, mechanical, and physical going forward. Ireland are physical in defence and very individual. France have this collective approach, eight men running at the same thing as hard as they can. If it is on the floor they will tread on it and if it is standing up they will shoulder charge it. Wales tend to do most of their stuff at close quarters and a lot of their aggressive play is underhand. France will put fingers in your eye and hands around your testicles whereas Wales will put a swift elbow straight in your face in a maul.

Biting has gone out of the game to a large degree because of the advent of gumshields. It is hard to bite anyone when your teeth are protected, and personally I would never go on to the pitch, training or for match play, without a shield. Some still resist their use and perhaps that is where the odd nip comes from.

Scotland are more controlled and work to put as many of their players in an off-side position as possible. They had a past master at this in Finlay Calder who would run off-side, put his hands over his head to indicate he had done so, and then walk back slowly between your scrum-half and fly-half, preventing the pass. The only player I have seen do something about Calder was Pierre Berbizier who deliberately threw the ball at him and won a penalty for off-side.

England go for power play in the forwards. Normally we have one of the biggest packs, and under Uttley's coaching, for example, we developed a driving, mauling game to set up the power players like Dean Richards and use him to drive forward. The back row in that year – Teague, Skinner, Winterbottom – gave us in Teague a player more geared to rucking rather than driving. He would move off, hit someone, and hold on until bigger support arrived and rucked over him. As Teague said, we were using the back row as battering rams to give the backs chances to run.

We were told in 1990, and at other times, that if our forwards won the ball all we had to do was ship it out and our world-class backs would score. That was patently not true. In all the games which England won when you look back on 1990 the forwards dominated the opposition to such an extent that you could almost guarantee between 60 and 70 per cent possession and it was on that percentage that the backs were able to achieve limited success – limited in comparison to the amount of ball they had. The England forwards would have liked the ball in their hands more. I think we could have achieved much more with it.

Scotland followed in our footsteps in fixture terms in 1990 and also picked up three wins in a row which meant that Murrayfield was to stage the classic confrontation come 17 March. The Grand Slam, the Championship title, the Triple Crown, and the Calcutta Cup were all up for grabs.

Heading North, the England forwards discussed the Scottish pack in detail. Many of our players had played with many of theirs on the Lions tour and we knew that we had to watch certain of their players. There was a lot of knowledge about each other, both ways, and a carry over from the Lions was that some players still had selection points to prove. The Scots, I heard, had not much appreciated Roger Uttley's coaching on the tour when it was obvious to me that Uttley's work with the forwards in Australia was vital in turning that tour around. In other words there were quite a few sub plots to the main event.

We stayed at Peebles, as usual, and the attitude struck me as too loose, too much of a holiday atmosphere, too much mucking around. I felt it was too relaxed, balls being spilled in training, and we all had some responsibility for that. We were going into a war zone and we needed to be switched on for that. It was strange to me because I felt that some of the players were not as keyed in as I was. After all, I had my private battle with Sole coming up and I had been giving him serious thought for three or four days, checking on the video what he and other Scottish forwards had tried against us before. Our final training session was fairly low key and Carling gave us a little of his motivation talk which was hardly necessary.

In the more detailed planning we concentrated on what to do about the Scots' back row – Calder, Jeffrey, and Derek White – and their generous use of the off-side law. What was needed was good scrum possession, retain the ball, then put a slight drive on to tie in the back row for a second. Then Teague would pick up and go, try to pull in one of the Scots centres, wait for the support to ruck the ball, and then push it wide, hoping for an overlap, or attack again on the same plan. We knew what we wanted to do from line-outs as well and I felt we were properly organised.

The atmosphere that day was said to be amazing, especially if you were a Scot, but to be truthful it passed me by. I know there is a lot of nationalism at Murrayfield these days and we received the usual reception which suggests the English are not popular. Out came Scotland led by Sole in a slow walk but it did not matter to me whether they walked out, ran out, crawled out, or came on a bus. It made no difference to us but it might have given them more sense of occasion if that was necessary. You have to remember that teams go out these days a long while before they kick off and all the posturing in the world as you come out can soon be eroded. What goes through my mind when I am out on the pitch before an international is straightforward. There is a wall of noise which you have to shut out to clear your thoughts, you have a look at your opposition number and say something to yourself like 'I'm going to have him' and that is about it.

Scotland took the wind, which turned out to be quite significant, and they kicked a couple of early penalties which was even more significant. The game started ferociously and the referee, David Bishop of New Zealand, penalised me after Sole collapsed into the tunnel at right angles. Dooley was behind me and I was pushed forward. I trod on Sole, the linesman saw it and flagged, and Bishop awarded a penalty and said to me: 'I know you didn't have any choice but if you tread on someone it's a penalty.' Craig Chalmers kicked that penalty and then another one when Ackford was penalised for throwing his handbag at Chris Gray.

The wind was strong and Hodgkinson turned down a penalty chance from halfway because he felt it was out of range. But we progressed to a situation where we had a scrum on their 10-metre line and from there we actually put our game plan into action and from the quick-rucked ball set up by Teague in came Guscott with a huge dummy to the Scots and over for a try. That was exactly as we had wanted. We drove on, creating a series of scrums close to their line as half-time approached and everyone in our tight five knew we had them rocking. We won a penalty on their line and when Carling came over Moore told him we had the taking of them in the scrum – give us another go. We tried again, and again Sole collapsed the scrum. The referee came to my side, spoke to the linesman, came back to the scrum and said to Sole: 'I know it is you collapsing the scrum, if you do it again there will be a penalty. Stop collapsing.'

We drove again, same effect, another penalty. This time Moore told Carling that if there was a repeat we were certain to get a penalty try. Another scrum, another penalty, but no penalty try. So we went for a back-row move but pushed out a poor ball and this series of great positions had produced no reward. I believe, and always will, that we should have had a penalty try in that period. But full credit to Sole who knew he was going backwards and would have conceded a pushover try and did what he had to do take the scrum down.

I do not know why Bishop did not award a penalty try. Maybe he thought he was in Scotland and the thought of doing so did not appeal to him. But I was not that concerned when we turned round at half-time 9–4 behind because I felt comfortable in what we were doing in the pack and the half-time chat reinforced our original planning. There was to be no change of strategy, no need to panic.

The Scots messed up the restart which meant a scrum back on halfway. It was a perfect scrum and we called a back-row move on Teague but in his haste he knocked the ball on. Scrum to Scotland. The Scots called a back-row move off Gary Armstrong and put Jeffrey through, then Armstrong again, and Gavin Hastings followed up with a wicked chip kick which bounced perfectly for Tony Stanger who scored.

It was now much more of a grind that lay ahead. The more the game went on, the more we drifted away from our game plan and the absence of Dean Richards, who had missed that Championship in its entirety after a shoulder operation and listened to that game on the radio while he was doing his police duty at a soccer match, began to tell. We needed Richards's size and power against a team which lives off-side and deliberately kills your fast ball. The more the game progressed, the more we beat ourselves. We had the evidence from 1988 to show us how to beat them but we played the wrong game, creating space out wide when we were confident as a group of forwards that we could take the game to them. Late on, when Carling was buried by the entire Scots back row on a switch play with Andrew, our chance had gone.

It was a bitter day and there were recriminations afterwards. So much hung on that game and we had been in a strong position for so much of the time. Victory should have been ours. I have never known a defeat to take so long to get out of the system and Scotland may never fully understand the motivation which has gone into succeeding matches against them. Murrayfield 1990, for all its disappointments, actually lifted and drove England into new pages of history. That was the net result of that afternoon's activities.

Chapter Nine

ALL THINGS ARGENTINE

I was never quite sure why England actually wanted to tour Argentina in 1990. If you went on the seven-match tour and looked like making it all the way through to the World Cup it just meant continuous rugby from one year to the next. For a while the England management seemed less than keen on the tour. Several players did not want to travel. So commitment was some way short of 100 per cent. On top of that, sporting links with Argentina at that time were still building up following the Falklands conflict in 1982 – and England were the first rugby team to go down there and build a bridge. There is no doubt that we were used as part of the diplomatic effort to restore relations between the two countries.

I knew that there had been one England tour to Argentina before, in 1981, when the boys had found the two Tests difficult going, and that in the seventies another tour planned down there had been called off by England because of guerrilla threats against the players. This time we travelled without Paul Ackford, Mike Teague, Dean Richards, Rob Andrew and Rory Underwood who said they wanted the summer off. We missed the experience of those players because their replacements did not have time to mature in a country where France and Australia have been beaten and even New Zealand have struggled.

The tour was based in Buenos Aires but we had three visits up country to play provincial opposition and see more of the hinterland and its people than we would have done if we had remained in the capital city. The president of the Rugby Union, Mike Pearey, a retired Royal Navy officer, was on tour with us and did not miss an opportunity to refer back to the Falklands and hope that all future contests between Britain and Argentina would be on the sporting field. As the presidents of the Welsh, Scottish and Irish Rugby Unions were on the trip as well I presume they agreed with our president's feelings.

Apart from the players who did not want to go to Argentina for a July–August mission, one who did but was left out was Paul Rendall. He was assured that his place was reasonably safe but I wondered if it was wise to make the trip without such an anchor man. I still took a view that the England forwards could achieve plenty on the tour. Perhaps my vision was coloured by the fact that we had had a good performance all the way through the Championship. We were still beating the Northern Hemisphere packs and I saw no reason why we could not do the same in Argentina.

All the planning and a fair degree of confidence went out of the window when we lost the first game 29–21 to Banco Nacion. The home team had a trump card in Hugo Porta who led them from fly-half. He is older than me but age was certainly no barrier as he scored 21 points and played a huge part in the victory. I did not play in the game but I sensed that things were not going to be all that easy from then on. Banco Nacion had sent a signal to all the other teams who were going to play us.

Will Carling and Geoff Cooke had to face up to the fact that the mission was going to be difficult. Carling had been used to Rob Andrew calling the moves from fly-half but now had to take more decisions himself and pass them on to whoever the replacement fly-half would be. Will began to look under pressure. Cooke read a mini riot act urging us to do things properly and maintain correct attitudes.

The second game was in a place called Tucuman against the local team. It was a bit of a contrast to Buenos Aires where our four-star hotel had every comfort. Life was a little more sparse up country with no television in the rooms of a fairly straightforward hotel. I have to admit that I will watch television whatever language it is in but I was even deprived of that. The ground we played on was basic and the dressing-rooms were worse. When we trained there we realised we would just have to put up with it, little realising that the ground and the people who would fill it were going to be a lot different at night. By the time we were ready to play, the people were seething with tension and the atmosphere was fairly intense.

Plenty of debris, oranges and harder things, were thrown at us when we came out of the underground tunnel on to the pitch, with armed guards watching. You could not help noticing that the Union Jack at one end of the ground was in flames, burned by the locals in what we were assured was a custom which was extended to all visitors. I took the scene in briefly but was more concerned about settling in with a new front row of John Olver and Jason Leonard than anything else. We needed to win badly to stabilise the tour and we did manage that – 19–14 after what seemed like hours of extra time from the referee to try to steer Tucuman into a situation where they could win. It did not happen, fortunately, and the crowd calmed down afterwards and started to show another side of their character by seeking our autographs, items of clothing, and tour knick-knacks. We had the post-match dinner about midnight, an affair enlivened by the tour doctor Terry Crystal doing a reasonable imitation of Max Bygraves on a table. I am not sure what the locals made of that.

The next two provincial games did not go our way even though there was only a score in our defeats to Buenos Aires and Mendoza. In the second game I was up against a kid prop named Federico Mendez with whom I was to have a closer acquaintance later that year. This time the refereeing was poor and everyone had to take care of himself against Mendoza whose win meant we had played four and lost three going into the first Test four days later.

I thought Carling was at a very low point. He was trying to find reasons why we were going wrong and why he was trying the wrong options. No one had done their selection chances much good in such a disappointing start but Carling seemed to feel that his position was being undermined by Brian Moore, the pack leader. Carling came into the room I was sharing with Olver in Buenos Aires and said as much, indicating that he thought Moore was overstating his role in the squad. We told Will that if it felt like that he should tell Moore himself but he never did. Moore won the hooking place in both Tests but Cooke switched the pack leadership from him to Winterbottom. Winters took that in his stride. 'I am the pack leader but unofficially Brian is,' he told us. Even so, on a tour where the results were not going our way, Moore must have known he was under pressure from Olver who had been sharp and was playing well.

Four new caps were chosen for the first Test. Leonard saw off the challenges of Victor Ubogu and Mark Linnett to win the loose-head place, aged 21, and Dean Ryan played at number eight. The two new backs were David Pears at fly-half and Nigel Heslop on the wing. All of us realised we had to raise our performances to beat Argentina, and as we headed for the Velez Sarsfield stadium you could sense that the tour was coming together. All the worrying had actually created a united force. Which was just as well. The Test was one of the dirtiest games I have played in.

In an early scrum we had just won the ball when one of the Argentine second-row forwards stood up and kicked me in the face, a most unfriendly act. Wade Dooley, who rarely misses a trick, saw exactly what happened but I told him not to worry and that I would sort it out as soon as I had the chance. I decided that the chance would come in the next scrum.

As we were about to engage I stood up and copied the Argentine's gesture by kicking him in the face and immediately he went to the ground, clutching his head and moaning. At this point the referee, Brian Kinsey of Australia, became involved. 'I knew you were going to get him,' he said, 'but I didn't think you were going to do it so quickly.' My view was that the Argentine had taken a liberty and would try it all day if he wasn't stopped. I was grateful I had a gumshield to save me from further punishment but the scar tissue from that match is still evident to this day.

We won the Test into the bargain. Simon Hodgkinson really did the business with the boot, scoring 17 points, to add to a couple of tries from my fellow Wasps, Dean Ryan and Chris Oti. What none of us knew at the time was that Dooley had taken a heavy blow into his ribs and was going to spend the next week trying to get himself in shape for the second and final Test.

We had a players' court after the Test, with Linnett as the Judge. Bob Kimmins, whose wife had given birth during the tour, was ordered to drink three bottles of champagne, one of which went down in 15 seconds. Carling, who was designated the court artist, was ordered to whiten the faces of Paul Hull, Chris Oti, and Victor Ubogu, all blacks, and that is how they went to the official reception until instructed to clean up. But the ice had been broken. Carling was relaxed for the first time on the tour. We celebrated – and waited for the final week to begin with a midweek game in Cordoba coming up next.

Olver was captain in Cordoba. Only one of the Test team was with him, none in the pack, which was a pity because it turned out to be a very physical farewell to the up-country games with the referee doing nothing to sort out Argentine indiscretions. Olver is never short of words and kept on at the referee to take control of one of the local forwards who was just out of order. Olver said he would take the team off if things did not improve but basically this was a fight with the ball. If it becomes open warfare you have no choice but to pitch in and Olver did just that, kicking the offending Argentine as he lay on the ground. The crowd, which started partisan, and worsened, did not like that at all. But the boys survived, held on, and gave us a base for the second Test.

But Argentina won the second Test 15–13 which was the first time they had beaten England anywhere. Dooley started the match but as luck would have it received another blow to his ribs and had to go off . . . when we were ahead 10–9. When you lose a man like Dooley things are bound to go against you – he had never gone off in a match before – and we just did not adjust fast enough when Dave Egerton took his place. Dooley went after 50 minutes but we were still in the game and could have won if Hodgkinson had retained his kicking boots from the first Test. We scored two tries but lost to five penalties from Vidou, the Argentine wing. Hodgkinson missed a couple of penalties and our chance had gone.

Another court session followed. In revenge for the black players who had been painted white, some white players had to be painted black. Carling was one of them and Cooke was not best pleased to see his captain and some players entering a formal reception in that condition. They were instructed to clean up, fast. Cooke felt the face-painting was wrong for our image. He was probably right but these things happen in the unique atmosphere of a rugby tour. For Carling it was just another factor in a tour which he could not have enjoyed. He was still very young and the pressures were hitting him.

Everyone did their own bit of self-analysis on the long journey back from that tour. I felt it had been a good mission for some of the youngsters like Leonard, Pears, Heslop, Ryan, and Tim Rodber. It was a bad tour for Kimmins, the huge Orrell lock who never really came again, and for Linnet who must have felt he would win a cap at loose-head prop but was overtaken by Leonard. As for Leonard, he was like a sponge, taking everything from everyone. He reacted to everything positive which he was told. It was a case of keeping him calm and keeping him thinking. I told him that if he stopped thinking he would stop playing.

I was not wrong about the Moore–Olver situation either. For our final two games in 1990, the first against the Barbarians and then the return with Argentina, Olver won the vote for hooker. For those of us who had looked and listened in Argentina it was an interesting little development, considering Moore's strong position in the side.

The Barbarians, celebrating their centenary, pushed us close at 18–16 but as a national side we just had to win, even though the Baa-Baas turned out a high-quality team exactly in their tradition for this first match against England. Argentina, though, presented us with the chance for retribution for that second Test defeat in Buenos Aires. They accepted an astonishing tour itinerary which had them playing Ireland, England, Scotland and the Barbarians on successive Saturdays, and not surprisingly they lost the lot.

The Argentines must have known they would have to be more disciplined once they came out of their own country and away from their own referees. They gave Porta the tour captaincy, at 39, and the coach was Porta's scrum-half from 15 years before, Luis Gradin. In other words, the men behind the Argentine squad when we visited them had been moved out.

The England match went completely our way. We won 51–nil and Hodgkinson set a new England scoring record with seven conversions and three penalties, totalling 23 points. England put in seven tries of which three came in the final eight minutes. One of them was scored by Jon Hall, the Bath back-row forward, who had not played for England since 1987. The match brought me up against Federico Mendez for the second time in the year. I knew that the 18-year-old schoolboy had had quite a match against Ireland the previous week and I found from the first scrum that he was so wound up that it would need little to push him over the top. He probably expected to have an easier game than he got. He is a very basic scrummager, lots of power and aggression, but no technique and that left him more frustrated as the match went on in its one-sided way. Given a few years the boy will be fantastic but here he could not control himself. We were into the last quarter of the game when we wheeled a scrum and they collapsed. We drove on and I stepped over Mendez as we did so. In his anxiety to do something to me he swung a fist at me and then grabbed towards my testicles. I trod on the side of his head and then we both fell over the other Argentine prop Diego Cash. As Mendez came up from the ground he curled his fist and lashed out at the first person he saw ahead of him which was Paul Ackford. As Ackford had his back to the boy he never saw the punch coming and it landed on the side of his face, putting him out cold. Exit Mendez, sent off by the referee, Steve Hilditch of Ireland.

The post-match dinner took place at Twickenham, and as is the custom at these affairs I sat with my opposite number, Mendez. He apologised for what had happened and I suggested to him that he became a little calmer and he would develop into a great prop. He had just been given a four-week ban for his offence and he claimed that he had been provoked – and that the provocation was my treading on him. He had dismissed the fact that he had tried to grab my testicles. On *Rugby Special* on television the next day the whole thing was shown in slow motion and bore out my version of events.

This did not prevent the Rugby Union deciding to take matters a little further. I was called before a three-man Rugby Union disciplinary meeting to discuss what had happened. We studied the video of the game all over again and no action was taken against me. At the time I was taking a little time out to play for England Classicals in the Bermuda Festival. The Rugby Union told me I could not even take part in that until I was cleared officially to do so. But one thing was certain – my contacts with Argentine rugby were at an end.

Chapter Ten

THE WORLD CUP STORY

Both Geoff Cooke and Roger Uttley looked for the positive aspects from 1990, building on the fact that we had scored 90 points, more than any team in the history of the Championship, and had gained record wins over France and Wales. Of course, said Cooke, the disappointment of not winning the Grand Slam was intense but he still believed that England could make a serious challenge in the World Cup in 1991 and that it would be more than valuable if we could win the Championship that year. It was vital, he said, to start off with a win at Cardiff.

The players could not have disagreed with Cooke. For my part I looked upon 1991 as the most exciting year I had ever faced, providing I stayed in the side. In many ways the English game was at a peak and if you could hold form, and stay free from injury there was a fair chance that you would have the most active year in rugby that any of us had ever known. Ahead lay the Championship, a tour to Australia and Fiji, and the World Cup. I defy any player to say that he did not have an expectant spring in his step at the prospect of staying in the reckoning all the way through. In Lanzarote, just ahead of going to Cardiff, I felt the vibrations, felt that people were drawing together as a natural development. But our time there was almost 100 per cent targeted on winning in Wales and the values that would bring to the rest of the year. Apparently the Welsh thought we were mad to go to a warm-weather camp to prepare for what might be a wet winter day at Cardiff but that missed the point. Lanzarote gave us perfect conditions to fine tune most of the plays which were to give us victory over Wales.

In the front row I was wondering what was going to happen to Rendall. Between Rendall and Leonard I believed that Rendall was still the better prop, but would he still be the best come World Cup time ten months later? I suspected that Cooke would run with Leonard until he got completely destroyed by someone giving him a bad experience and then switch back to Rendall and hope he would last out. I was convinced in my mind that Leonard would continue and I phoned Rendall and told him so. Paul made his own choice to keep going and rightly made the World Cup squad. But he was never first choice again – he had one game in the World Cup, against Italy, when he replaced me after injury, and that was the last time.

Lanzarote was physically hard, as hard as I had known, and there were casualties because Jon Hall damaged a knee so badly that his come-back attempt which had looked so promising came to a halt. There were other less serious bumps and Cooke delayed announcing the side to face Wales as a result. The other residents of the Club La Santa included the Olympic sprinter Merlene Ottey and as her training gear used to be hung on a line close to our living area it was no surprise when a couple of our players appeared in it one evening as we sat by the bar, did a lap of honour around the square, and disappeared. I often wondered whether Merlene Ottey thought she was wearing sails after that.

Eventually Cooke announced a side which was to play unchanged through the Championship, the first time that had happened for 31 years. Uttley was now in his planned final year as coach and he seemed to need some reassurance that he was still up to the job. I noticed this in Argentina and I noticed it again at the start of 1991. 'Am I giving enough?' he would ask you. I had always felt that Roger was brilliant in coaching a style of play without ever deeply analysing the opposition. In his fourth year as coach we had become accustomed to his routines and I believe as a group of players we had gone beyond his limits. Consciously or not, we made our own minds up about what we were going to do. I suppose we were being selfish about it but the need was for analysis rather than tactical suggestions.

Cardiff loomed. We had our final training session at home at Gloucester, scrummaging against the club pack which was a hard exercise conducted in front of one of the most knowledgeable but one-sided crowds in the game. They gave us stick. We probably deserved it but we had to go on to Wales and the Gloucester pack didn't. Cooke had decided there would be no more fringing on the outskirts of Cardiff for the Welsh game – we went straight to the middle of the city, plunging ourselves into the people, taking all the jibes. I was more concerned about taking the cheap shots, off the ball stuff, which Wales were capable of putting in to break the rhythm of a side. I was one of those appointed blocker at kick-offs to provide a protective shield and as it turned out Wales did spend a lot of time kicking off. Wales are not alone in testing the limit of the law – everyone does because international rugby produces situations where you live on the edge in every single phase. That is what makes it entertaining and people look for those moments and it is the reason why players test the referee and see what they can get away with.

Ray Megson, back on the Cardiff stage for Wales–England after a four-year gap, penalised us very early and Paul Thorburn slotted the kick to put Wales in front but I did not feel intimidated by that or by being in the Arms Park as a player for the first time. In fact Leonard and I were the only two England players who had not been on that pitch before and we shared the confidence of the rest that we had this match for the taking. As a pack of forwards we could take the game to Wales and hold it there. It was not a matter of over-confidence but one of belief. The backs played to our strengths up front and drove us on, highlighting the understanding. It may not have been very attractive but it was the means to an important end. Hodgkinson had a mighty day with the boot with seven penalties and the one try we scored, fortuitously through Teague who had missed out on all but a few seconds of the 1989 game, demonstrated our absolute control up front. It meant, of course, that all the years without England winning at Cardiff had come to an end and if we made all the players who had been there since 1963 and not come up with the goods feel a degree happier then we had done a job. It was 25–6 to us, no argument.

The Cardiff Silence followed. Nobody went to a press conference, which is usually held after major matches, which meant that Cooke and Carling were read the riot act by the Rugby Union because going to those conferences was part of their duties. We had a team meeting that evening and it was agreed that we were not refusing to talk but wanted to let the effects of the game settle in, allowing us to collect our thoughts. We needed to assess our point of view at being the first winners there from England in 28 years. It was a side issue that there were some negotiations going on about fees for interviews. The silence did not have a great deal to do with that and it was short lived anyway. We had done the business against a Welsh side which had been in decline for a couple of years but which still believed it could win. We did Welsh rugby a massive favour; they were shattered by that result and have started to do something about it.

A month was a long while to wait to play Scotland who, we assumed, thought they had taken over the mantle of the Welsh as the team which beats England more than it loses to them. But surely Scotland could not have miscalculated how much we needed to win that game. With many players the Murrayfield result had become an obsession and had to be wiped out at the next opportunity especially as the World Cup permutations suggested we would be playing Scotland later in the year. This was a time to state our case.

I was surprised that Scotland chose to seek a forward confrontation which suited us ideally. There was tension in the first scrum and Sole appeared to try to hit me but landed one on Moore instead and that scrum broke up into a fight. There were no verbals, just so much tension, and the game went along on a fair number of penalty kicks, five to Hodgkinson for England and four to Chalmers for Scotland, until Nigel Heslop scored the only try, from Hodgkinson's neat pass, and we were on the way to victory by 21–12.

The London Nautical School squad of 1973–74. Jeff Probyn is second from right, front row

Darryl Druce, then captain of Old Albanians, lines up with his men. Jeff Probyn is second from right, back row

Wade Dooley on the ground, Jeff Probyn in the centre of the picture, and Nigel Redman on the right, are checking what Dean Richards is going to do with the ball in the 1988 England trial at Twickenham (Express Newspapers)

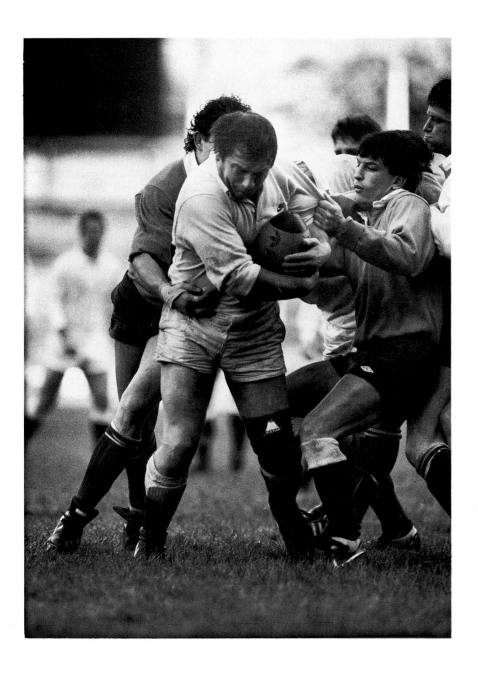

The 1988 England trial at Twickenham with Richard Harding of Bristol, who captained the England B XV to victory over the England XV, tugging at Jeff Probyn's shirt (Express Newspapers)

Both feet off the ground, Jeff Probyn high steps it at Twickenham at an England training session (Roy Chaplin, Express Newspapers)

A break from training – Jeff Probyn relaxes during a session at Twickenham (Express Newspapers)

The Judge at work. Paul Rendall holds the ball tight despite the intervention of an Australian arm and the imminent arrival of Jeff Miller, the Australian flanker, in the England v Australia match at Twickenham, 1988 (Express Newspapers)

*The World squad which toured South Africa in 1989 smile (mostly) for the camera.
Jeff Probyn and Paul Rendall are top left, back row*

*England v Ireland at Twickenham, 1990, was Jeff Probyn's day with the ball in
his hands. He scored the first try in England's 23–0 win (Express Newspapers)*

The finished product. Jeff Probyn, plus elegant polished cabinet, ready to set off on a delivery (Express Newspapers)

Ireland gave us a massive fright in Dublin. It was as torrid as usual over there with England trying to impose and Ireland coming at us from all angles to disrupt but when Simon Geoghegan popped over in the corner for a try early in the second half and we were 7–3 behind, winning the Triple Crown, let alone the Grand Slam, began to seem enormously difficult. The word went around the pack to keep grafting, keep believing, and not to panic. So we dug in and drove on and Underwood put us in front with a fine piece of midfield running and finishing and just to top it off Teague scored his second try of the Championship and that match was in the bag 16–7. Meanwhile France whacked Wales 36–3 on the same afternoon and for a second year the final round of the Championship was between two unbeaten sides, England and France.

For this game there was not the overwhelming optimism of the decider a year earlier. We looked at this game rationally, knew we were going to face an aggressive, powerful and technically sound pack and backs who would shoot all over the place if we let them. We had no intention of playing a fast and risky game and knew that our control and discipline would have to see us through. It was a case of preparing for the unexpected and knowing that when France had the ball the nearest player had to be tackled. They are the best ball handlers in the Northern Hemisphere and we had to stop them gaining momentum. This was brought home to me quite vividly by a good-luck telegram from Pierre Berbizier who was going to play scrum-half for France. 'Ball, ball, ball,' he reminded me, just as he did when we were in South Africa together.

On the morning of the game I looked around the forwards at the team meeting and could see the resolution that was going to bring a win. There was a calmness which came from the assurance that we knew exactly what we were going to do and that persisted all the way into the dressing-room and out on to the pitch. I was the oldest player in what was now an experienced side and I knew this day was going to be special to me and the rest of the team.

The match will be remembered as the day England won the Grand Slam for the first time for 23 years and for one of the greatest French tries ever. Hodgkinson started us off with a penalty in the first minute but when he missed one not long afterwards, hitting the ball towards the south-west corner, Berbizier came into play with his 'ball, ball, ball' theme. We had actually gifted the ball to him and even though he was behind his own line he had plans. He held the ball behind his back as the England forwards drifted right for a drop-out and set off parallel with the goal line, heading to our left. Berbizier linked with Serge Blanco, playing his 85th game and final Championship match, and the escape became fact. Lafond and Camberabero injected more pace and found more space and Sella came next. Camberabero returned, chipped over Underwood and re-gathered, and then hammered over a cross kick. All this was being played out in front of our grasping fingers and anxious minds. We could not reach them because the whole thing had happened too fast and the ball was doing the work. 'Ball, ball, ball,' said Berbizier. And that ball came from Camberabero's boot towards Saint-Andre who gathered on the bounce and scored.

We had the best of the rest of the first half and turned round 18–9 up after Andrew dropped a goal, Hodgkinson kicked two penalties, and Underwood had scored the only England try when Hodgkinson provided the extra man. That 18–9 score looked nothing like enough and the precious gap we needed was obtained with a fourth and final penalty by Hodgkinson. Still France kept coming and two more tries had them within range at 21–19 and what seemed like an hour to play. It was nothing like that, of course, but three minutes in that situation can seem like a lifetime and slowly we played out the seconds until we won.

The reaction of the players and the crowd is something I will never forget . . . it was a marvellous, magical time of celebration and just sheer relief all round that we had done it. I had come to a Grand Slam in my fourth season in the side and you had to feel deeply for those who had been there longer – Winterbottom from 1982, Underwood, Hill and Teague from 1984, and Dooley and Andrew from 1985. Surely, they felt, as I now did, that we had a side to go forward to the World Cup and be a real threat. Cooke must have felt that too because that Slam was a triumph for the squad and its methods and preparation. Cooke could argue that now we had something to show for our scientific approach. We had proved consistency under a management which had set individual test programmes within a team framework. The Grand Slam could be looked upon in the changing world of rugby as a positive step forward.

Personally, I relaxed too much between the end of the Championship and the England tour to Australia which followed that summer. I had enjoyed myself with my family and in the pre-tour tests Gary Pearce had better ratings than me. But my body was saying that I was doing the right thing in easing up and I knew I was capable of playing on that tour and fulfilling what was asked of me. The management slapped my wrist by not choosing me for the opening game against New South Wales but Pearce had to drop out with an ankle injury and I played after all. We lost the game but Cooke and Uttley both went out of their way to comment that it was one of the best matches I had played in an England shirt.

Yet Uttley was watching me and wanted me fitter. Pearce played three games in a row, the third of which was against Fiji B in Lautoka, and during this first stage in Fiji, Uttley stopped the team bus three miles from our hotel and made me run back with him, not a pleasant experience in that heat, but I got the message. Uttley was even more concerned about Dooley who had punched one of the Queensland team and suffered a broken bone in his hand as a result. Dooley missed the last four games of the tour including the internationals against Fiji and Australia – which opened the door for a newcomer, Martin Bayfield, to win his first cap. Dooley was not the only important absentee against Fiji because Ackford withdrew as well with an ankle injury which meant we had an entirely new second-row pair, Bayfield and Nigel Redman. After my own experiences on the tour I was just glad to be selected, no matter who was behind me, and we managed to turn a trip which had not been going too well on its head with a 28–12 win. Fiji have these big, strong guys who look as through they train by shifting pianos but no longer have the discipline to compete at the top and will have to revise their thinking if they want to. This particular day in Suva found them wanting to set the world drop-goal record and their fly-half Serevi fired them from all parts of the pitch but landed just one. I scored a try, a fine running effort from all of three yards out after Bayfield had put in a good drive but it was Rob Andrew's first ever try for England which actually settled it – he followed up his own kick to score. We had a long celebration that night and not long before dawn found some musical instruments left lying around by the band, still plugged in to the sound system. This was too much of a temptation for the lads and we made our kind of music until Cooke was called to quieten us down. We all scattered except Redman on the drums who was duly read the riot act the following morning, which was not all that far away.

We returned to Australia. This meant a pre-Test match against the Emerging Wallabies at Gosford where Simon Halliday was kicked around the eye by one of their props, the only bad moment in a strong performance by what was then the second team. The boys had won, it was the end of their particular tour, and the singing was loud and continuous on the coach journey to Sydney where we were based. Carling objected to the singing because he wanted to watch a video on the coach system but this view was greeted with derision. Richards went forward to Carling and asked him to leave the lads alone and let them sing. Carling seemed upset by this and in a later discussion with Richards said he felt that his authority as captain had been undermined. But Richards stuck to his opinion that it was the end of a tour for one group of players, that we had won two games in a row, and everyone felt the lads should unwind – and in the end Carling agreed with him.

Australia took us on at the Sydney Football Stadium almost at the top of their game. They had stuck 63 points on Wales a week earlier and although we knew there was no way we would concede that number of points we had to work hard chasing them to keep the margin down to 40–15. They ran in five tries and although we attempted to play a wide handling game they were a bit sharper at being off-side and obstructing us, and although we created opportunities we did not come up with sufficient scores. The back-row pace the Wallabies generated was impressive and gave us plenty to think about if we were to meet them in the World Cup. However, there were little bonuses because Bayfield had now come through two Tests and discovered more about himself and we had twice had a good look at Willie Ofahengaue, the Tongan tank in the Aussie back row. I kept saying to myself that the loss of Dooley was as critical to us as it always had been. That Test against Australia took place on 27 July and there was no escaping the fact now that our next assignment was the start of the World Cup against New Zealand at Twickenham on 3 October. When Cooke named his squad, there were no surprises, no uncapped players, just a group of 26 players who were able to recognise their own abilities and the abilities of those around them. On the tour Webb had displaced Hodgkinson at full-back in a change that was to stick and end Hodgkinson's involvement as a regular choice.

We had been told for a good many years how good New Zealand were – and this game was a watershed. We had their greatness rammed into us over and over again, that they were an awesome winning machine, not men, but supermen. We had countless videos of their training to illustrate tackling, mauling, rucking and commitment over a long period of time, and it did condition us to thinking that we were going to come up against this mighty machine which was unbeatable. You cannot remove a picture which had been put into your head over the previous four or five years and of course so few of us had actually played against them – a mistake of timing and contact which should never be repeated. All of our coaches even went down there to look at the patterns and try to build them into the English game. It created an aura of expectation which was not realised. The All Blacks did not live up to their billing. And we lacked a certain amount of self-belief, maybe because we had lost in Australia or maybe because the management stressed too often that we might be big fishes in the Northern Hemisphere but here we were up against the Southern Hemisphere and the country which had won the first World Cup. The All Blacks were physically better equipped than we were but not as emphatic as we had been led to believe. They beat us 18–12 but it proved to me that they did not have the supremacy we had heard about and that if we had gone on to play them again in the final we would not fear them. There was no longer a mental block.

Steve McDowell was opposite me for the All Blacks. I knew a lot about him, that he had been playing for them since 1985, that he was a black belt at judo, and that he was rated highly. He came out with his left sleeve cut off which said to me that one of the New

Zealand supermen was bothered about playing against me. The last person in the world I expected to see opposite me with his shirt cut was a New Zealand front-row forward and I realised that he had been thinking about me, watching videos to see how I played, and what he thought would work against me. That in itself was quite a nice feeling. He is a strong scrummager, technically different in that I had never played against a guy like him. He tried to come outside me and stand up, forcing me upwards, taking my right arm and pushing it backwards. If you kept him tucked up he could not do it and the scrum was quite comfortable. I like to think we squeezed them a bit.

I took more notice of the noise the All Blacks made. Everything which happened brought this chorus of noise – 'Look, ref, he's holding the ball', or 'Look, ref, he's off-side', and so on. All the time they were telling the referee, Jim Fleming of Scotland in this case, how the game should be played and there is no doubt this has an effect on the referee. Referees are intimidated by the great New Zealand name. You can see it is part of their tactics – and sides which are coached by New Zealanders do the same. Northampton are great talkers and so are London Irish. Both have New Zealand coaches and I am sure New Zealanders use the referee as part of the game, draw his attention to things that happen to them, not to the things they do. They cast doubt in a referee's mind about an event even if it looks alright. The referee may not react to that incident but he could react next time. It also puts doubt in your mind as a player. You could be running and hear 'Ref, knock on, knock on' and that could slow you down. You half check, thinking the referee might blow. Good referees are not affected by it but the tactic exists. When you have the ball you do not expect the amount of noise which comes at you. Nobody had warned us but other teams will develop it if they believe it will work for them. The Australians already have.

At least the first match was out of the way and I had the satisfaction of being a World Cup player at last. McDowell and myself swapped shirts and had a chat afterwards, both of us in agreement that we were glad to get the first game out of the way. I had his All Blacks shirt for a while but it was stolen during the competition. If you see someone wearing a shirt without a left sleeve, give me a call.

The defeat to New Zealand confirmed what we would have to do late on in the competition – face France in Paris in the quarter-final and Scotland at Murrayfield in the semi-final. We had to beat Italy and the USA to qualify but did that without too much difficulty. I stretched medial ligaments in a knee against Italy and had to come off and face treatment for ten days – which gave me time to read the *Heinz Guide to Rugby* which was given away with match programmes. Props, I was intrigued to read, are rugged, when on your side, and violent thugs when playing for the opposition. They pant heavily and usually stand bent over, grasping the front of their shorts. They are known for biting each other's ears and shaking hands after the game. Well, that's what it said.

We had team meetings continually to assess what we were doing and where we were going and during one of these at our base in Tylney Hall in Hampshire Carling said it was time for an open and frank discussion with all the players – without any fear of retribution. Even though we were winning we were being criticised for not being as adventurous as we were in 1990, for example, and Carling clearly felt this criticism. His theme was that if we had the amount of penalties awarded to us which we had against Italy he wanted a team consensus on what we should do, kick or run. He ran through all the players who were there and to a man they said take the points, kick for goal. Carling surprised me by saying we should run the ball from penalties and it took a great deal of arguing before he agreed with us. The rest of us wanted to run only when we were a long way in front. He gave in.

En route to Paris we had a couple of days in Jersey with our wives or girlfriends which was an astute thing to do on Cooke's part because it broke up the divide between touring while being at home and being on the road. We celebrated the fact we had come this far and that was good for team spirit. We wound down almost completely and it was a key factor in building the attitude we needed to play France. The worst problem on any tour is boredom and the Cup campaign had now become a tour involving a group of individuals who may not pick each other for company by choice but are thrown together. As a father I did not want to be away from home but as an England player I had no choice. International rugby means you play in a once-in-a-lifetime event and you never know when it may be your last game. You are part of the rugby business and are a commodity within that. If someone decides you are not the right commodity you are on your way. So my philosophy has always been to seize the moment.

Parc des Princes was becoming familiar to me. We lined up in the tunnel, France stretched away on our left, referee David Bishop in between, waiting to go out and everyone was steaming. I could not wait to break into the wall of noise outside and get going into the game which promised to be huge. There was so much for both teams to play for in this one-off game which would either point us to Twickenham, our ground, for the final or leave us to go back to work on the Monday.

Blanco, a god-like figure in the French game, was on a farewell to rugby if France lost. We wanted to catch Blanco with the ball and roll him over in numbers which we managed to do. We put in another up and under which Blanco marked but the referee was slow in calling it and Heslop hit Blanco with a tackle. Blanco hit Heslop and Eric Champ planted a haymaker on the Orrell wing which probably caused mild concussion. This was an example of the intimidation that was coming from us and France came back on an entirely different tack by hitting Leonard time and again. They knew it was a waste of effort hitting me but there was plenty going on elsewhere. As usual with France it was professionally done but there were no innocent parties on either side. Their stuff was well hidden but when Winterbottom kicked Cecillon in the head it was highlighted as dirty England at work. We knew that if we continued to frustrate them they would lose concentration – but there was a lot going on. To a certain extent the game overtook the referee because it was difficult for him to see everything. But there was no sending off, no serious injury, and the penalty count was in our favour. We outscored France on tries two to one and won 19–10.

The significant alteration that the management had made for the French game was in the back row. Richards was stood down from number eight, Teague moved across, and Skinner came in at tight flanker. Skinner is a classic big hitter and went around looking for the moment when he could lift the game with one of his crunching tackles. He had his chance when Cecillon broke from scrum and Skinner waited there, arms ready, shoulder dipped, legs ready for the drive, and put Cecillon back about eight yards in a devastating piece of individual play. Skinner took his chance well, as he always did, and he took his own character on to the pitch to demonstrate his defiance. I was never sure if Cooke and Skinner were on the same wavelength but as Skinner lives his life on the edge I doubt it. It was a tough decision for Richards to have to accept and could have been explained to him more fully by Carling who must have known what the management were doing.

There was said to be trouble in the tunnel afterwards between Daniel Dubroca, the French coach, and the referee but I did not see it. Obviously French pride was hurt because as 1987 runners-up they saw their destiny as making the final again, if not winning it. I just sat in that rather austere dressing-room letting the feelings of victory run through me before we commenced a night of serious celebration. We met with some of the French players much later on and about 3.00 a.m. I set off finally for out hotel and, to my surprise, I asked directions from a man walking along with a baboon on the end of a chain.

Now we knew we were in the World Cup almost to the death, whatever happened against Scotland. If we lost the semi-final at Murrayfield we would still have to play a third-place match against either Australia or New Zealand. But we had our sights set on beating Scotland and winning a place in the final.

We went straight to the middle of Edinburgh for the run in to the semi-final and I sought a little relaxation in a shooting party in the Highlands with Teague, Richards, Olver and Morris. The most experienced at this activity was Olver who kept telling us about the number of shoots he had been on. But very late in the day up popped a couple of pheasants and Teague was struck in the head by some shot from Olver. It was a flesh wound but we decided to keep the affair totally quiet because we thought that Cooke would ban any kind of recreational activity if he found out. Teague had to sit in team meetings with his hand covering the mark on his head. We had got off to an explosive start.

The 1990 match was played to us again on video more as a reminder that we had to carry the battle to Scotland and sit on them. Carling gave us some motivational chat, hardly necessary at that stage because the objective was so clear. Each player in the England side had his personal targets to achieve and mine, once again, was to take on Sole and prove I was better. At that point I had no need to be motivated and the talking bored me. I just knew that there had never been a time since I came into the squad when I could relax in the knowledge that I was going to be picked. This was because of my age and the fact that I did not see eye to eye with everything the captain and management wanted and I had been known to voice my opinion.

We had captured public imagination by making the semi-finals at the expense of France where many thought we would go out. But we had come through with style and the right mental attitude and the profile of the team was going higher and higher. The expectation in the country had risen, we knew we were not going to let it go against Scotland, and how could we let down the millions in England who wanted us in the final? How could we let anyone else play on our ground?

Scotland had to be denied possession and having created an identity as a pack and a complete respect for each other we were at a mental peak. The Scottish fans showed their dislike of us which was another factor in our preparation. If you are in hostile surroundings it gives you even more determination. We won 9–6 and could so easily have lost if Gavin Hastings had kicked a penalty for Scotland at 6–6. But the proof up front was that we dominated, we went for pushovers, and we should have had a penalty try when Paul Burnell collapsed the scrum and dived in. Sole was just not in the game and it was probably the easiest game I had had against him. I suspected he would miss not having Kenny Milne at hooker and I was right. John Allan is a competent hooker but he is not a scrummaging hooker and Sole spent all his time going backwards. We drove them in five-metre scrums on their line even when Sole tried to take the scrum down because we could push him up and keep going. Burnell did his job and hung in there for his life which kept Scotland in the game. But no one could argue with our domination which was 60 per cent plus of the ball coming our way. It relied in the end on a dropped goal from Rob Andrew to win it. And if the Scots wanted to blame Gavin Hastings that was cruelly wrong – they had lost it long before his miss.

We headed for Twickenham and home, pausing at a leisure complex in Grantham on the way for another family reunion and some relaxation. I rated that another good move by Cooke. My second son, Steve, called in and beat me at golf and Skinner entertained all the children who were around with his version of water games and for a while our minds came off the main issue of facing Australia in the final – the Aussies having beaten New Zealand 16–6 in the Dublin semi-final.

The Aussie propaganda machine, led by David Campese who loves giving England a fair amount of stick, suggested we were a poor team incapable of changing styles and opening up. But we decided to stick with our regular policy and damn the criticism because if we won everyone would forget the style and remember the victory. The basis of our game would be to attack from 30 to 40 yards out. Australia's nagging did not find any favour with the players but I am sure it put pressure on Carling and Cooke in the days before the final. Obviously there was some discussion, if not dissent, among the backs about the way we were heading. Carling asked the backs why we were not running it more and Hill said to him that he was captain and if he wanted to change things then he should. It was Carling's responsibility and he had to take it, Hill said.

There was no mistaking the significance of the final even if the distribution of tickets meant that the crowd lacked the communal punch of the committed thousands who attend Twickenham for Championship matches. This was a one-off, in all respects, led by the presence of the Queen. The Princess Royal, patron of the Scottish Rugby Union, was also presented to the teams and Brian Moore could not resist saying 'Sorry about last week.' In some ways the Princess Royal was one of the spurs to our win at Murrayfield, seeing her in her tartan, her children in tartan, and singing *Flower of Scotland*. It gives you a bit of a buzz to see that royal patronage has taken a turn for the nationalists. Of course the Scotland team were at the final as well, wearing kilts and Australian scarves. We could see them clearly from the pitch and if we expected support from another of the home countries we could see that it was not forthcoming. Perhaps the Scots despise the England team because we have figured out how to beat them, consistently.

England dominated much of the final and had about 75 per cent possession. We had enough of the match to win but we made mistakes, sometimes under pressure, sometimes not. The Australians scored the only try, driving Tony Daly over from a line-out, and won 12–6. It was still there for us at half-time when the question was: Why are we not sticking to the game plan? Why are we not playing the percentage rugby that we set out to do? We all agreed – the Aussies were ready to go. We won the rucks but the Aussies had players out to concentrate on defence. They needed to be tied in by a series of forward drives to prove the value of our tactics and we did not put in enough of them. The Aussies read what we were doing and put bodies all over the pitch to stop us running. Carling should have brought the game back to the way we intended to play rather than kept running against that Aussie wall. We still created opportunities and one of them brought Campese into our line to knock on deliberately a ball which would almost certainly have brought a try for Underwood. In such a match, all or nothing, I do not think any player would hold it against Campese for doing what he did. Effectively he guaranteed Australia the World Cup.

If someone had said way back at the start that we would reach the final and lose it 12–6 having dominated so much of the game, I think we would have said 'great, that would be enough'. But having got there and played the game, the feeling afterwards was one of total depression. There were no recriminations or time for any. We had to thank our supporters and then we went to the dressing-room for perhaps 40 minutes of quiet time. The eight-week climax to months and months of preparation was over. It was a while before I realised the enormity of what we had achieved – winning in Paris, winning in Edinburgh, and providing a final which was worth watching because we were the only team to play rugby on the day. Australia contributed little and were guilty of the things they had accused us of doing which is a fine irony.

I tend not to dwell on losing. It was gone, we could change nothing. There was a fine, relaxing dinner afterwards with players from the four teams who had made the semi-finals all present. I laughed along with Daly, the prop opposite me, who had cut off his sleeve and covered his arm in Vaseline as a counter to me and he said it had not worked. I kept the shirt which I wore in the final. It means no more or less than any other I have worn on England's behalf. But I knew I would never have the chance again – and that shirt is staying with me.

Chapter Eleven

THE ASKEAN
CONNECTION

One of the things which I did not expect to come under strain in World Cup year was my connection with Wasps. I know people accuse me of shopping around a little for my club rugby but the fact remains that I joined Wasps in 1984 and am there still. But if you turn up the World Cup programmes for the games which England played you will see that I am listed as a player with Askeans, the Kent club, as is Paul Rendall.

Before the World Cup Rendall had decided that he would not be playing for Wasps for much longer and was looking around for an opportunity to play for and coach a side outside the First Division. Evidently Askeans heard of his objectives and talked to him about it. It is fair to say that Wasps had had a hard time in terms of coaching in the 1989–90 season under Mark Taylor, a New Zealander, who took a curious stance if you were not available for the club because you were on duty for England. He responded to that by trying to leave you out in the next game for which you were available and seemed to have no understanding of the fact that international players, and not just those from England, have to regulate their games. This applies particularly during the Five Nations Championship but is also true at other times because demands are growing season by season.

Taylor left Wasps and Rob Smith, who succeeded him as coach, said that with the World Cup coming up Rendall and myself would not be around until November and might only fit one or two games in between the end of the World Cup and the start of the 1992 Five Nations matches. Smith said we would not be concerned for club rugby and that as Wasps had won the Courage League title for 1989–90 he wanted a settled team.

Wasps had won the title on the last day of the season. Gloucester needed to win at Nottingham to be sure of the title. But they lost. Meanwhile we beat Saracens at Sudbury and that was enough to make Wasps champions, with nine wins out of 11 matches. They gave us a replica trophy – the real one was at Nottingham – but no one objected to that. We were and still are the only London club to win the title. But this had a different effect on different people and Smith felt that Rendall and myself would not be committed to the club because of the World Cup and that younger players should be brought on.

I understood what Smith was saying and while not necessarily agreeing with it I could see that he had a point. I knew that Rendall had decided to look at the option of being player–coach to Askeans who had finished the previous season at fifth place in the Third Division and decided that I would look at the club as well. Geographically Askeans were closer to my home than Wasps and at that stage it did seem pointless to put in all the miles driving to and from Wasps only to be guaranteed a place in the second team.

What we were talking about was an eight-game segment which I would miss at Wasps but could play at Askeans. I spoke to the chairman of Askeans, Alan Eastwood, and said I could play eight league games for them but would return to Wasps the following season. This would give Rendall the advantage of having an experienced player with him at Askeans and together we could give Rendall some help up the coaching ladder which was then completely untried for him.

Next we had to tell Wasps of our intentions. My view was that under the circumstances I saw no point in my playing in the Wasps second team. There was no way I was going to leave to go to our immediate First Division neighbours, Saracens, and whatever was thought at the time that was never an issue. I pointed out to Wasps that the nearest League clubs to me were Blackheath, then near the bottom of the Second Division, and Askeans – both a relatively quick drive through the Blackwall Tunnel under the River Thames. Wasps wanted the whole business kept quiet for a while, which I agreed to, but the player-registration business had to be adhered to and it was when this was done and I was on tour with England in Australia that the news came out.

To me changing clubs for a season and going from First Division to Third Division was no big deal anyway. I saw no way that it would affect my fitness or ability to challenge for an England place. After all, Wade Dooley had been doing exactly the same thing successfully while playing for Preston Grasshoppers, also from the Third Division. The World Cup period was also unique in the game in Britain. Clubs would have to take a back seat . . . at least for the first part of the season.

As soon as it became public that Rendall and myself were heading for Askeans, based at Kidbrooke in Kent, the rumours started that as current England players we were being paid handsomely to make the switch. The figure said to be involved grew as fast as the rumours. We were being paid £15,000 to join Askeans, with more to come depending on results. But there was no money on offer from Askeans. The inference was that we had moved for money but in Rendall's case he was looking to downgrade his rugby a bit and move on to coaching and play at a different level. I am his mate and decided to go with him.

The twin forces of the Rugby Union and the press were now ranged against us. Askeans were placed under relentless pressure by both of these organisations and there were times when I wondered if there was more importance being placed on this than on the World Cup which was about to follow. Askeans subjected themselves to a thorough investigation and maintained throughout that all the allegations which were made against them were baseless. I felt in the end that I owed them something, not the other way round. I played precisely one game for Askeans. Rendall tore his Achilles tendon during the World Cup and did not play for them at all. Rendall was the main reason for my going to Askeans and when he withdrew I decided not to go ahead as well. But I did want to put in a game for them. I was getting nothing out of the whole operation except a lot of flak but I could put up with that. So I told Askeans I would play.

I went through the World Cup listed as an Askean, even though I had not made an appearance for them. Two weeks after the World Cup final I was on a train to Leeds with Askeans to play a League match against Headingley – opponents who Askeans had never beaten. I had just spent week after week with the England World Cup squad, literally being on tour in my home country, and I really did feel a stranger in the camp as the Askeans travelled north. I realised I did not know a single player in the team I was about to play in. It was an unusual feeling, not helped by the fact that I knew nothing about Headingley either. In seven years at Wasps I had not come across either the team I was going to play for or the opposition. I was out of context that day at Headingley.

It was not a special game and I did not have to play hard. I scored a try, which was satisfying because I have not had many of those at any level. I also found that I could virtually control the way the game was played. There was plenty of enthusiasm among my temporary team-mates but no direction. For example, I would try to set up a rolling maul but Askeans had never played one so that foundered. It was just 15 guys running around, nothing structured, and I found myself thinking that Wasps would have won every game at this level of English rugby by 40 or 50 points.

In the scrums we won the ball against the head whenever we wanted. After we had scored a try from one strike the referee came up alongside me and said: 'Jeff, would you take it easy on your opposite number so that they can win a ball and make a game of it.' This was only about halfway through the first half and I thought it was a request which insulted the players I was playing with and those I was playing against. I carried on playing the same way and I knew what the next move would be. I had to stop playing my way and go through the motions otherwise I would have been penalised out of sight.

On the train on the way back to London I decided not to continue with Askeans and told them so during the journey. I thought about it for a while and that was it. I returned to Wasps and played eight games in the second team while I re-qualified for League rugby. I suppose one of the reasons why I left Askeans so quickly was that I was not attuned to club rugby of any sort after the World Cup and the step down was so dramatic, playing with guys who did not play the way I expected the game to be played. Mentally I was not ready for it. I have no wish to sound conceited, it is just that at the top it is an entirely different game and perhaps I did not think it through beforehand.

I have had a few clubs in my time but until this one all of my moves had been in what I considered to be an upward direction. This was my first move downwards and I did not enjoy the experience. I still play outside the First Division, at Wanstead perhaps on a Sunday or for a pub team, but in League rugby you have to take a firm commitment on to the field as well as your ability. I effectively coasted the game that day at Headingley because I was able to put the brakes on mentally and physically. Maybe I should have given Askeans a longer run but time has told me I made the right decision.

I know that during my brief association with Askeans they clinched a couple of sponsorship deals which may have had something to do with my being there. And I hope I can go back there with some advice in future years because I will not play on for ever once I am out of international rugby. I might become a forward coach somewhere but I am not looking to be a full-time coaching administrator.

There was a time when I came close to joining Harlequins. I was not happy with the way Mark Taylor operated his system of keeping you out of the first team even if you had been away with England, and Quins made it quite clear that I could have a first-team place with them. The disenchantment lingered for a while but the fact that I did not move to Quins shows that the situation sorted itself out.

Chapter Twelve

SLAM AND OUT

On the morning after the World Cup final a strange sense of reality came over us. The Cup was decided, the party, and yes it was some party through that Saturday night, was most definitely over. While the lads were at the official dinner, the Rugby Union entertained our wives and girlfriends in another hotel and we linked up later. No expense was spared in giving us all a great finale. We were putting our relationships with each other as players on hold for a while except in the case of Paul Ackford who was definitely pulling out of international football, having said to himself that when England were out of the World Cup he would go. The same applied to Roger Uttley as coach and I felt he had less input at the end of his four years than he did at the beginning.

I was in no mood to dwell on the World Cup now that it was over. I went back to work on the Monday morning which must have pleased the other nine people I work with considering how long I had been away. Not many people at work know much about rugby, in fact not many in my business know much about it. It was time to get on with life as a family man and a man with a business to run. Already I was one of yesterday's heroes and it had probably cost my company £2,400 to pay for the two men who stood in for me while I was away with England. I was not alone in losing money. Jason Leonard did. So did Paul Rendall who finished the World Cup on crutches after snapping his Achilles tendon packing down against the scrummaging machine. It happened during the last part of one of the final training sessions before the World Cup ended. We had done some live scrummaging and then went in against the machine. Uttley wanted Rendall to have a couple of scrums and in he went with us, down against the pressure, into a good locking position and then there was a noise as if someone had clapped their hands. Ackford likened it to hearing a piano wire breaking, lots of pings and then a final snap. Rendall hobbled off and had to have an immediate operation. This may sound a little harsh but it was a good way for him to end his international career. He did not have to make the decision to retire and after being involved for a number of years he was not slowly discarded. His pride would not let him retire in 1990 when it was clear he would not be picked as first choice again and when he still knew he was up there as one of the best. He was hurt against the machine but providing there are plenty of rubber springs there is not much damage you can do to yourself. Most machines help you to improve technique. They are not that good for teaching you how to scrummage because unlike people they do not move around. They help to improve timing and technique on drives but as soon as you start putting pneumatics on to these machines you can create all sorts of problems. If you have any minor injuries, the machine will expose and worsen them. Rendall had had a calf-muscle problem earlier and may have been lacking elasticity.

When that machine comes back at you there is something equivalent to a ton pushing at you as the compressed-air rams react to you hitting it. The rams control not only the forward positioning of the contact pads but move them up and down as well. Ideally, when the front row hits the pads you want to keep them down and pressed in. If the rams came back at you and lift at the same time and you have the second row locked in well behind you, it is easy to see that your back can arch quite severely. The props have to take that strain, both ways. I remember going in against one of these machines for the first time and when the pressure came on I did what I do in a normal scrum, looked to turn away from where the pressure was coming. Phil Keith-Roach, a former London hooker who was part of the development team, said to me: 'You can't do that, Jeff. You are in a rigid area and can't lose the pads.' The only way I lost the pads was to go underneath them. So there is no real way to get away from the pressure and if you have got it wrong you have a lot of problems. The way I scrum against a machine is completely different to the way I scrum against other players. You can scrummage as the books say with both feet back because at the end of the day the machine is not going to collapse and you are not going to fall on the top of your head. If you have your feet back in a live scrum and it collapses you have nothing to stop you heading for the floor. Kids who are taught to scrum against machines could get injuries because of what I have described. They should learn to scrum against people and learn the safety aspects first. Technique and timing and all the other business can come later. A machine is great once you know how to scrummage and know the pitfalls and dangers of being in the wrong position.

England packs have scrummaged brilliantly against the machine but not been up to par on the pitch and I would always insist on preparing against a live pack. Machines have been around for a while and it is not easy to generalise because a machine which suits the England pack would be of little use to Old Albanians. When the England pack goes against the machine we actually have a guy from the manufacturers to set the parameters on the system. There are technically able guys all around, on and off the machine. I doubt that you could create that in every single club.

Jason Leonard's neck problems, which subsequently required an operation from which he recovered so well that his international rugby was uninterrupted, began in the late stages of the World Cup and continued through the 1992 Championship. He had a compression injury in which a disc had been moved slightly and then crushed. No one can say for sure how that started and what caused the injury to develop and worsen but it is a fact that it happened. In a natural scrum,

Leonard, as a loose-head, would have less pressure going through his body than I would. Things got so bad for him that in the last game of the Championship against Wales he could not bind and I had to bind his arm in. On our put in I bind over the top and he binds underneath and we reverse that on the opposition put in. In that match he bound underneath all the time so I could hold his arm in place. We knew this before we went out and were well prepared as a result but if a scrum had collapsed in a particular way Jason could have ended up seriously injured. Jason's right arm had withered and he had lost something like an inch-and-a-half of muscle as a direct result of the pressure on his nerve. I do not blame players for wanting to play but in many instances they need to be protected from themselves, and managers and coaches at whatever level have to play a part in that. Jason had intensive physiotherapy before and after matches during the Championship because he had little feeling in his arms. We were all aware he had a problem and I would have been happy for him to have a year off after his operation. But there were targets he wanted to play for like the Lions tour and you cannot stop players trying for those targets. There was a great carrot and he took the risk to play for it and came out on top.

The management decided that we did not need warm-weather training after the World Cup and nobody disagreed with that. Ackford had gone and Bayfield was there to replace him, but we lost the smoothness and assurance of using Ackford and Dooley simply because Bayfield is 6ft 10ins and having him at the front of the line-out gives us a height problem to be overcome and really there was no solution. The opposition defend the front of the line-out which makes throws to the middle all that more difficult. This was one of the things for Dick Best to consider now that he was the full England coach in succession to Uttley – and I am sure that Best would agree he inherited a strong, well-organised side which played through to a second Grand Slam in a very laid-back way. Best did not have to do a lot except continue the old system. His great asset is in telling us what the opposition will do and devising tortuous training for us. But in his first season this was not forthcoming.

For the Championship we reverted to our 'old' England shirt while the Rugby Union sorted out an agreement for the future with the manufacturer, Cotton Traders, and on the pitch we went back to our old winning ways with a 25–7 win at Murrayfield. It was strange to see a Scottish team without Jeffrey and Calder and the men who succeeded them were not in the same league. Of more interest to me was the return of Kenny Milne at hooker, because I knew he would improve their scrummaging, and it was also to be the last time I faced Sole. Milne was upset and caused a bit of a fracas when he was kneed in the face – but it was Sole's knee that did it. This was also the game where Dooley took flak for punching Doddie Weir in the ear, off the ball, but everyone on the critical side conveniently forgot that in a previous line-out Weir threw a superb right hand and hit Dooley on the side of the face as he went up for the ball. Dooley, being the sort of guy he is, sought retribution as soon as he could and it came after a 22 drop out in full view of thousands. Weir has never complained and clearly realised that if you throw them you get them back.

Much worse, mentally, was the pushover try Scotland pulled off against us at a five-metre scrum. It was the biggest blow to my personal pride and it resulted from a combination of factors after a stoppage because Moore was injured. We reformed and were set to engage when Scotland charged in and as they did so we stepped back and were looking for the referee, Derek Bevan, to re-set the scrum, which is standard practice. But this time, as Scotland gained a nudge of forward motion, their scrum-half Andy Nicol fed the second row. We were already going over the goal line and dropped the scrum, too late as it turned out. The referee had allowed the charge, allowed the crooked feed, and on that basis it was no surprise when he allowed the pushover try. We were not at all happy but it was the spur we needed to raise our game because we knew in our hearts that Scotland were not capable of pushing us over without everything dropping in their favour as it did then. They whooped a bit at the score, which was to be expected, but we spent the rest of the game pushing them around, taking them apart. We ran in tries from Rory Underwood and Morris who was back at scrum-half after a three-year gap and saw the Scots look anguished when Richards replaced the injured Rodber after an hour. Some substitute!

Ireland caught a backlash from us at Twickenham because we scored in the first minute with a try from Jon Webb, scored six tries in all and ran away with the game 38–9. That score makes it sound ridiculously one sided but Ireland, to be fair, were well in the game in terms of basic possession but had nothing like the same quality in their ball users. Webb scored 22 points to equal an ancient England record and we played some sound combined rugby.

Moving on to France, we reasoned that this was now the team which could stop us taking a second Slam and the peculiar thing about the match in Paris was that it proceeded much as we had hoped until virtually everything we had done was overshadowed by the sheer mayhem in the final few minutes. There had been a lot of pre-match conjecture that France would lose their discipline. Some of that conjecture was fuelled by Moore who heightened his profile and became the dream of the media men in predicting a war at Parc des Princes and aggravating a situation which still bore a resemblance to the World Cup quarter-final. As France had picked three players for their tight five from the hard school of the Begles club it seemed that they wanted to counter fire with fire in spite of coach Berbizier saying he expected his forwards to control themselves. I tried to keep my own mind in low key. I did not think it would be in French interests to get this hard image up and running and thought that they should play the game with their usual ferocity but within the law. Moore's words may have helped to sell newspapers but did not give the team preparation or the game any major service. Moore was also putting himself up as a target because France could figure he was trying to do something to them. We wanted to go in with control, as usual, and on their ground it was probable that something would crack. Quite early, Moore's head popped out of a scrum and a finger was stuck in his eye, Moore looked at the touch judge for sympathy but got none, and a pattern had been set. Jeff Tordo, the flanker, was the most aggravating person in the French team and put in most of the cheap shots, late arrivals to rucks to punch the guys on the side or drop in with the knee and look to elbow you on the side of the head. Despite all this, France played well.

There were a couple of fine tries for both sides but in the second half we were putting the pressure on and feeling we could win. We put in two big drives in a scrum, they collapsed, and the referee, Steve Hilditch of Ireland, awarded a penalty try. The French argued that we were not moving the scrum forward when it collapsed but in reality we had not really started to push them. The collapse was obvious and the penalty-try decision justified but it served only to add to the tension. The French forwards were still putting plenty around and when Bayfield was caught on the ground Gregoire Lascube, the French prop who had been opposite me all the match, did something really stupid and stamped on his head. Compared to some of the other things which had gone on this was not that bad but it had been in full view of the touch judge and there was no argument – Lascube was sent off.

The next few minutes went by without scrums so the French loss was not put to the test. But when a scrum arrived, Tordo moved in to hooker and the original hooker, Vincent Moscato, moved to loose-head prop, opposing me. Tordo was nagging at Moscato who seemed to lose all control and it was obvious they were going to have a pop at me. Without knowing the language, I could see I was being targeted, the positions of their heads said so because they were going to close the gap I wanted to go into. This was no problem for me because I ducked a little lower than usual and Moscato caught his nose on the top of my head. This upset him even more, the scrum broke up, and the referee told me not to retaliate and I said: 'I'm OK but you better keep him calm.' Hilditch called in the French number eight, van Heerden, who is bilingual, and the message was relayed to Moscato – calm down, and leave a space for Probyn to go into. Hilditch said later that Moscato was up with the birds and sure enough he went for me in the next scrum with another head butt. Once more I ducked and the scrum broke up in fist-fighting. I kept my head down, as always, because you stand less chance of getting hit that way and put a few punches back. Richards came to my rescue, pushing Moscato off, and the referee moved in fast to send Moscato off. I knew I was blameless and in control of myself while Moscato had lost control and his team lost the game 31–13.

We played on and Tordo was fortunate to remain. As far as he was concerned it was now open warfare and Moore was going to get it from him. Tordo seemed to seek him out at every ruck and maul which followed, no matter how much we tried to shield Moore.

Moore told me that if the game broke up again that I was to hold him back because he felt on the verge of losing his control. He was aware that he was at the end of his tether and if he was sent off he faced being banned from the last game of the Championship. Everyone knew he had given the match a fair old build-up in the press. No one wants to be sent off and here France had completely blown it with the loss of two players. I have been sent off a few times in my career and learned the lesson – four weeks banned for retaliation playing for Richmond against London New Zealand, eight weeks banned for provocation playing for Richmond against Wasps, and four weeks banned for retaliation playing for Richmond against Bridgwater. I was meant to have some brain power as well an A level in biology, four O levels and two years as a litigation clerk in my teens. So I knew what rugby's laws meant and I knew how France had suffered that day. Hilditch had a reputation as a timid referee and we had a certain amount of dread at facing a physically hard game. But he coped with every demand thrown at him. I know we came off best but you have to remember that intimidation is often a two-way street. There are no angels in the English side, but we are no more violent than many other sides and a lot less than some of them. If you play as a controlled unit you can dish out punishment without infringing the rules.

Two weeks later our back-to-back Slam became a reality – the first since 1924 – when we beat Wales 24–nil. Wales came to Twickenham on a mission of damage limitation. They just wanted to survive with the minimun number of points scored against them. They did not want to play much rugby and certainly did not want us to play any rugby, and for much of the game were reasonably successful in making their targets. Dooley won his 50th cap that afternoon and not only led us out but scored the last of our three ties, and Webb ended up with 67 points for the Championship, a record. In scoring 118 points in the four games we passed the record of 102 set by Wales in 1976. But if the first Grand Slam was overwhelming the second was underwhelming, something of an anti-climax if that was possible in a season where so much had happened. In some ways it was an easy campaign because we were still on a high from the World Cup and had taken that intensity into the Championship. The levels of commitment had been set in the World Cup and then maintained and the break before the Championship had enabled us to put the Cup defeat out of our systems and start afresh.

The Rugby Union arranged an end-of-season celebration dinner in London's West End. The players were given a gold sovereign and embossed gold cuff links and wives and girlfriends a gold half sovereign. And if you were the wife or girlfriend of a player who had completed all eight matches in the two Grand Slams you received a silver rose as well. These were pleasant gestures by the Rugby Union and probably expensive ones too and as far as the World Cup players were concerned could be added to the gold medals we were given for coming second – the champions Australia received platinum medals to the same value. Our backroom boys received mementoes from the Rugby Union as well – which included Kevin Murphy, the team physiotherapist who is rarely recognised publicly but does the most to keep the players on the field. When managers and coaches might give up on you he would carry on through the night to make sure that you were fit to play. I remember in Australia in 1988 that Moore had a problem with a fallen arch, the doctor had given up on him and he was in danger of going home. But Kevin designed a support with padding and strapping and Moore was able to go to a fitness session and pass it and stay on the tour. I stretched my medial ligament once playing against the Northern Division and Kevin, who was working for the North that day, nipped in with ice and his track suit top and hands at work to put me on the way to recovery. I was fit after four weeks, a week ahead of an England selection deadline for what turned out to be the year I won my first cap. They have given an OBE to Will Carling and an OBE to Geoff Cooke – and I would like to see an OBE go to Kevin Murphy as well.

Murphy's work has helped me and many others but I believe I am alone in having expensive dental work paid for by the Rugby Union. I damaged my teeth playing in a representative game, London v North, when Micky Skinner dived to try to tackle Tony Underwood and hit me instead, and then playing against Ireland with Jim McCoy's boot in my face. In all, three teeth were affected and I now have a bridge courtesy of the Rugby Union and put in place by a dentist who is a hockey player and knows a lot about injuries to the mouth. He also supplied me with a special gumshield costing £150 which is made of a flexible substance which absorbs impacts and helps to prevent concussion. No mouthguard can give you 100 per cent protection because if you are hit hard enough something will give. But this one helps.

The summer of 1992 was a dead time because England had no commitments – but there was a fitness session looming in September and a game against Leicester which was planned to warm us up for the match against Canada at Wembley. I knew I was not at a fitness peak but it was still a month before we played Canada and I was quite certain that I was building up properly. On the bleep test, I was higher than Victor Ubogu in spite of the fact that I was almost ten years his senior. But at the next England training weekend Cooke told me ahead of the team announcement that I was on the bench for the Canada game and of course I soon found out that Ubogu was at tight–head.

I had not been on the bench since 1989 but took a positive attitude and went ahead as a spectator against Canada without taking too much notice of the fact that this was the first and probably the last time England would ever play at Wembley Stadium – the switch was made necessary because Twickenham was being altered on the East stand side. I watched the scrums closely and knew that against Canada's big pack and quality opposition they had not gone as well for England as they should have done. Yet afterwards people were saying to me that I would be back in against South Africa and I was so sure that I would not be that I took on two £50 bets with a pair of journalists whose judgment was out of tune with their wallets. I won the bets because I knew that Cooke would be reluctant to change but he dangled a carrot for me by naming me in the England B team against South Africa at Bristol. I had not been in this team for three years and it would have been easy to say that enough was enough and not give it full commitment. But I soon dismissed that thought and Cooke assured the side that there were places still available in the England team. That game also brought me under the coaching of Jack Rowell of Bath for the first time and I was impressed. He had something of the style and approach of Alan Davies. He was analytical and looked for weakness in the opposition but still concentrated on what we were going to do as a team. I was happy with the work we put in on unit skills and with the ball work and felt we could do well against the big South African pack which was coming in on the back of a tour of France. We scrummaged well and were not driven backwards but lost to a couple of tries which reflected on bad defence on our part. It was still a close match and I was reasonably confident of making the actual Test the following Saturday. But it was not to be.

Ubogu remained in the side, I remained on the bench, and England beat South Africa. I did not believe that Ubogu was the right player to replace me and if I was out for good I considered that Andy Mullins, given a year or two, would be the best choice but I still had confidence in my own abilities. Anyone who was coming in for me had to be 100 per cent committed to enjoying being in the front row. You have actually got to like being in there and if physically you dislike it you will never be any good. How many guys have gone into a second row and said they did not like it because it rubbed their ears? Others go in and enjoy the physical aspect of the second row. If you are going to be a successful tight-head basically you have to like being a pain in the arse. Because that is what the job is. Tight-head props are like midges around you when you are fishing, like a traffic warden who waits by the meter for the expired time sign to flash up, they are people who annoy, disrupt, and mess you around. Loose-head props have to enjoy facing that and working out how to beat it. I contend that Ubogu does not like scrummaging but will do it if pushed. Mullins, on the other hand, has a certain skill level which is improving.

None of this stopped me congratulating Ubogu and I wished him luck and told him what I thought the South African front row would be up to. There was no escaping the importance of the day to South Africa after all their years away and their president F.W.de Klerk was in the crowd to mark the return. I sat in the front of the stand with the rest of the England bench and it amused me to be behind a sporting crowd who chanted out: 'Don't worry, Jeff, you will be back.' And when England went back in an early scrum they chorussed to Cooke: 'Get him off, get Probyn on.' Stuart Barnes, benching it alongside me, said I was the only one in the stadium who was smiling as England had a hard first hour up against it. The truth is that the England scrum did not go well and the other aspects which Ubogu was supposed to bring to the game did not manifest themselves. He was picked for his running around the pitch, which he can do very well, but this was international rugby where you get little space or time on the ball. The basic scrummaging job had to come first and anything after that is a bonus. You cannot artificially manufacture situations in training as we did, with Ubogu out in the centre of the field ready to run, and expect that to work against a team as big and well organised as South Africa.

England won quite well in the end, 33–16, against a tiring South African team but several elements had not gone well and I was sure that Cooke would have been aware of them. For me, though, a golden opportunity beckoned because the Barbarians put me in their line-up against Australia who were to complete their tour of Ireland and Wales with a one-off game at Twickenham. This was good news after being on the bench for England and having to hear the man who replaced me ask me afterwards, 'Jeff, what was I doing wrong?' This was slightly embarrassing because, as I have stressed before, I felt I was the better player and like all international players I had to have that inner belief. I advised Victor to look at the positive things and build from there. There is a strange unwritten law with props that goes along these lines: if you hammer someone you still say he is not a bad prop and if you are hammered yourself you never admit to it but just say the opponent was OK. So never gloat, never make a mountain out of your setbacks. Both props know what has gone on and talking to other people about it does not serve any point. The players around you know what has gone on as well and if the pack is shunted around the field the players will know what has caused it. Victor will have learned and I hope he goes in aggressively to his scrums rather than defensively.

The Barbarians did me a big favour by putting me in against the world champions and the tight five was the usual unpredictable mixture – Nick Popplewell of Ireland and Nigel Meek of Wales in the front row, and Norman Hadley of Canada and Ian Jones of New Zealand at lock. I had not been in with any of these players before but we sorted a few things out at our first training session, or loosener might be a better description, and then went to London to watch a

Jeff Probyn and Jeremy Guscott link up during an England training session (Jack Kay, Express Newspapers)

Richard Hill fires out a pass during an England training session with Jeff Probyn, right, heading in too late to lend a hand (Express Newspapers)

The Judge at training. Paul Rendall puts in the effort at home on a rowing machine, one of the pieces of equipment introduced by England in the eighties to improve fitness (Jack Kay, Express Newspaper)

On with the pads. Wade Dooley tries to create his own brand of mayhem against Will Carling and Jeff Probyn at a training session

Dressed for the camera, minus gumshields and support tapes, Jeff Probyn, Brian Moore and Jason Leonard rest easy (Express Newspapers)

Dressed for modelling, Jeff Probyn, Brian Moore and Jason Leonard demonstrate the new England strip (Jack Kay, Express Newspapers)

Ready for action. Jeff Probyn, Brian Moore, and Jason Leonard, with the rest of the England pack, prepare to work on the scrummaging machine (Express Newspapers)

Brian Moore (left), with Peter Winterbottom (behind) and Will Carling, pause during an England training session (Express Newspapers)

World Cup action. Brian Moore signals his delight as England score in Paris during the 19–10 quarter-final win over France in 1991 (Express Newspapers)

World Cup action. Jeff Probyn (right) checks what is happening as Richard Hill (number nine) attempts to halt a Scotland attack in the semi-final at Murrayfield in 1991 (Express Newspapers)

Grand Slam form by the England forwards with Dean Richards driving at Mike Hall of Wales in the last match of the 1992 Slam at Twickenham with Wade Dooley and Peter Winterbotton about to lend support and Neil Jenkins ready to intervene for Wales (David Spurdens, Sunday Express)

A little commercial activity for Brian Moore, Will Carling and Jeff Probyn for one of the sponsors of the Run with the Ball campaign (Express Newspapers)

More drills for the England forwards with Peter Winterbottom, Jason Leonard, Wade Dooley, Martin Bayfield and Jeff Probyn waiting for the ball to arrive in an England training session, 1993 (Express Newspapers)

Halting the French. Jeff Probyn and Jason Leonard try to prevent the French breaking away at Twickenham, 1993 (Express Newspapers)

Will Carling in pensive mood during the 1993 Championship during which England lost two matches, the worst record in the five Championships under his captaincy since 1989 (Express Newspapers)

performance of *Joseph and the Amazing Technicolour Dreamcoat*, followed by dinner in Carnaby Street. I do not know what all the kids queuing up to see Philip Schofield thought about all these craggy rugby men heading into the theatre but 'Stormin' Norm' Hadley was so impressed he bought the CD. For a Thursday evening we had a big binge, a lot of drinking games, and by the time we were back at our base at the Lensbury Club in Teddington we all knew each other a lot better. As a group of players we got on well which is a major step towards playing a game like that when you are always likely to come second.

The Australians put out basically their Test side and we fought them all the way without coming close to winning – the score was 30–20. My front-row colleagues were determined that one of us would score a try and from a tap penalty move where I was the allotted ball carrier I saw that the Aussies had fanned out and went from close in for the line. I was driven over by Meek and Popplewell after riding a couple of tackles. In view of everything which had gone on in the previous few weeks that was one of my happiest moments anytime, anywhere. There was this nagging certainty inside me that I might not get an England call again and this might easily have been my last game at Twickenham with all that the ground meant to me. To score under the posts in what could have been perceived as my last game was a great sensation. The crowd applauded me all the way back to my own half and for a prop forward that is something which does not happen very often. The other guys in the team were equally generous and congratulated me because they knew the value of that score. That match had been a unique high point and I believed I had shown under the revised laws that I had not let anyone down, that my style was not disruptive to the common cause, and that I blended in with players I did not know. I had been given the chance to advertise myself.

So a mixed year came to an end, highs and lows, darks and lights, and it left me thinking of all the players I had been with for England and all the key men I had faced. When I ran through my best team of opposing players I started with Steve McDowell of New Zealand at loose-head, the best I have been up against, and alongside him I saw the Australian captain Phil Kearns and on the other side was that wily and compact Argentine, Diego Cash. In the second row I would play Olivier Roumat of France and Bob Norster of Wales and ask them to move around the line-out a bit and make people think. I would play Marc Cecillon and Laurent Rodriguez of France in the back row and Finlay Calder of Scotland at number seven because he was immense at playing off-side and breaking down so many attacks. I would play Robert Jones of Wales at scrum-half and make him captain and give him Franck Mesnel of France as his partner. My centres would be Scott Gibbs of Wales (of whom we are going to hear so much) and my mate from France, Philippe Sella. David Campese of Australia and Ieuan Evans of Wales would be my wings with Serge Blanco of France at full-back.

I have tried to pick my best 15 for England – but failed, which may amuse Geoff Cooke. I cannot settle on who should be at fly-half, Rob Andrew or Stuart Barnes, so I would recommend them for different games and differing circumstances. Put Andrew into a tighter game. Barnes into a loose one. My full-back is Simon Hodgkinson and my wings are Rory Underwood and Mark Bailey. My centres are Simon Halliday who is the more complete player than Will Carling and has the vision to bring out everything in Jerry Guscott as he showed on their only England pairing together in 1989 against Romania. My scrum-half is Nigel Melville, the most complete footballer in the number nine shirt in my time, and I would make him captain as well.

My pack will surprise no one. I go for the men who have been through the fires with me and back again a few times and more – Micky Skinner, Peter Winterbottom and Dean Richards, Paul Ackford and Wade Dooley, and Brian Moore and Paul Rendall in the front row, hopefully with myself.

Chapter Thirteen

GEOFF COOKE – MY VIEW

The two men who have managed England in my time in the squad are Mike Weston and Geoff Cooke. I cannot claim Weston as a mate because he took me all the way to Australia and back for the 1987 World Cup without offering me a cap, and as he was the English selector for the British Lions tour to Australia in 1989 I presume he did not support me for that venture either because I was not chosen.

Weston, unlike Cooke, had a long history of involvement with England when he became the first manager – everyone else in that role had been titled chairman of selectors. But in 1985 Weston was made manager all the way through to the first World Cup. I have been told that Weston did not want the England job to be his show and that he laid the emphasis on players, coaches, and selectors.

Weston set about changing things for the players who had been saying for years that the Rugby Union gave them a raw deal in terms of just being friendly to the players who attracted full houses to Twickenham and elsewhere. Weston increased ticket allocations to players, brought their wives and girlfriends into the hospitality circle which accompanies all main games, and generally made the players feel more wanted. For the first time we had formal England clothing and leisure wear off the pitch. All of this was a breakthrough.

Weston acknowledged that the fitness levels of England players had to improve and introduced monitoring and personal fitness programmes which all of today's players accept without question. He went to Australia well ahead of the World Cup and put together a sensible package of activities on and off the field, including an away-from-it-all break at Hamilton Island off the Queensland coast which the players appreciated.

From my standpoint I felt that as long as Weston was involved in running the show I would not be picked. He did not choose me when the other tight-head prop, Gary Pearce, was injured during the World Cup so it was clear to me there was something about my style of play which did not appeal to him. I was also sure that Weston did not want to give first caps to anyone during the World Cup unless he had to, and the only player who came into that category was Jon Webb at full-back when Marcus Rose was injured in the first game, against Australia.

Before we went to the World Cup I am sure that the incidents at Cardiff which led to four England players being suspended for one match affected Weston deeply. The rest of the players in the squad thought it was wrong that those suspensions were applied and Weston came to me and said: 'You boys don't know what I have been through. They wanted to ban the lot of you and I said I would resign if that was the case.'

I do not believe that Weston was the sort of person to enforce his will on people; he was one to ride along with the current of things, and he did not take real control of the squad. He was more in the background, as he always suggested he should be. He was happy to leave his coaches, Martin Green and Des Seabrook, to look after things during the World Cup, and even though Weston thought he should have had one more year after the World Cup, the Rugby Union did not see things his way and he went.

I had not met Geoff Cooke before his appointment and knew little about him beyond the fact that he had played and coached in the north of England and his highest coaching post was as coach to the

Northern Division. My lack of knowledge of Cooke was balanced by the fact that I knew his choice of coach, Roger Uttley, extremely well. Even now, six years on, I would say that the forwards have had little to do with Cooke. Geoff was a three-quarter himself and when he first appeared at training sessions, track-suited as he had promised, he worked with the backs. That was the area where he wanted to have an influence and probably he knew very little about forward play.

Cooke inherited an England trial from the old regime and that took place early in 1988 which is the first time I heard him speak at length on his plans for the English game. I was in the senior side in the trial, which we lost, but Cooke and his co-selectors, Roger Uttley and John Elliot, decided I should continue and win my first cap against France in Paris. Elliot was the one survivor from the Weston regime, the silent one of the new trio so to speak. Elliot had asked me in Australia where I thought I was going next and I told him that I would play for England one day because in my view I was better than the other guys around and I was determined I was going to do it. When it came to my moving forward with the backing of Cooke and Uttley, Elliot would have known of my determination and Uttley would have known of my physical capabilities. At that stage I do not see how Cooke could have known much about me.

Cooke was a new broom that winter and appeared to be looking to make changes in the side. But there were not that many because Will Carling and Micky Skinner were the only other new caps against France with me. Cooke came across to everyone as a man with ideas and his approach to the job was more professional than Weston's. He grasped the nettle with both hands and in the matter of fitness, which had already become scientific and athletically based, moved it on still further. Weston had seen the need to raise levels and Cooke wanted them raised again. Cooke decided early on that he would keep the hard core of the side together which was a strong indication of his professional attitude. We found out that he analysed us and analysed the opposition in just about equal measure and the reason he did that was to improve our mental attitude.

He is very switched on to success and does not deal with failure all that well. For example, when we were in Argentina in 1990 on a tour which did not go particularly well he was poor in that he did not let the players unwind when results were bad. One area where players can unwind on tour is in 'court' sessions where various misdemeanours, real and imaginary, are dealt with and punished in some horrendous ways. All good fun, all player orientated, and an excellent buffer between a match and the formal functions which usually follow. But he banned these sessions in Argentina while the team was losing. In my view that was no way to run a touring side. You need lighter moments, it cannot be serious all the time.

Because the players performed so consistently, Cooke has not had that much experience of defeat but the ones which hurt him hurt us as well. They range from Wales in 1989, Scotland in 1990, New Zealand and Australia in the 1991 World Cup, and then Wales and Ireland in 1993. All of these defeats came during a time when Cooke was able to keep his best players on the field almost as often as he wanted. But he has a habit of tinkering with the team unnecessarily and in some ways has probably caused us defeats by doing it. He has excluded players for no apparent reason over the years – why were Mark Bailey and Nigel Heslop, both natural wings, dropped for Simon Halliday who was a centre? Why was Dean Richards dropped for Mike Teague during the World Cup? Why was Richard Hill dropped for Dewi Morris when he had done everything which had been asked of him in terms of passing out almost every ball he received from the forwards.

If England win, Cooke is happy and smiles and is keen to get on with doing the bits and pieces of management which go hand in hand with big matches. If we lose, like the players he is reasonably quiet. I believe he looks for scapegoats in defeat and there are lots of players who have received video tapes from him pointing out their mistakes. I am also convinced that there are other players who make mistakes who never receive a critical tape, Will Carling being one of them. I have yet to receive a tape. In his own mind I am sure he had had an elite set of players who are untouchable – Peter Winterbottom, Will Carling, Rory Underwood, Jason Leonard, Brian Moore, Jeremy Guscott, and, until recently, Rob Andrew. These are key players who he would not look to criticise or remove.

I do not think Cooke is particularly visionary but we will be able to judge that better by the time the 1995 World Cup is over. By then some of the experienced players who have been with England even before Cooke came in will have moved on naturally. He faces crucial decision-making in the pack – perhaps only four of the 1993 pack will go through to 1995. The 1995 back line might not alter much but there are so many good centres around pressing their claims that it will be interesting to see how Cooke deals with them. I look at Nick Beal, Damian Hopley, Phil de Glanville, Graeme Childs, and Gavin Thompson, and I see five players pushing for centre places. There may be others. I just wish there was the same number of players pushing for the second row.

Rob Andrew was dropped after the Welsh match at Cardiff in 1993 and I am not at all sure he should have been. Why make him the scapegoat? From the players' point of view it was the biggest surprise in Cooke's regime. None of us expected it. I felt that losing in Wales was not necessarily Rob's fault. It was almost as if Cooke dropped Rob to prove himself right. Rob did not play particularly badly against Wales – a lot of the poorer areas of our play were not so much to do with Rob but with Dewi Morris inside him which created pressure. Will Carling dropped a lot of ball in that game but there was no chance of him being dropped. As for Dean Richards, if you ask anyone else in the world to name an England pack the first name they would come up with is Dean Richards. Everyone would start with him. If you asked the England forwards to name an England pack they would all begin with Dean.

I believe Cooke tinkered when he did not have to as if he had to do something to show that he was managing the side. It could also be part of his psychological approach to the game, to keep players on their toes and make them aware that almost anyone could easily be left out. He is professional and I am sure that to him players are commodities. He is almost like a football manager, which in a way is a compliment because it underlines the professional attitude which he brings to the game.

But it is not so good for players. Cooke is talked about as a great communicator but in my case I do not agree. When I was left out against Fiji in 1989, for instance, the way I found out was when I had a letter congratulating me on selection for England B. Not a word from the manager about what I had done wrong, why I had been left out. I was moved aside without so much as a by your leave. I know they came back to me because the player they brought in did not perform as they wanted. It would still have been constructive to tell me why I was out. It was just the same earlier that year when I was fit and available to play against Romania but left on the bench in favour of Gareth Chilcott who is a good prop without doubt but not of my calibre on my side of the scrum. He was basically a loose-head who could double at tight-head if pushed. After we had lost the Grand Slam decider in Scotland in 1990, Cooke was absolutely correct not to drop players. He must have realised, as we did, that there was more to come from the team despite the numbing loss to Scotland and of course we went on to better things in 1992 with very few alterations. I was next left out in 1992 against Canada and South Africa, again without explanation. In fact Cooke told me I was on the bench against Canada when we met in a car park during a training session shortly before the game. I could accept not playing against Canada because I saw that as a chance to experiment. But quite naturally I wanted to play against South Africa on their return to England for the first time since 1969–70. Again I made the B team against them. Again, no explanation.

Whenever I have gone to Cooke to find where I stand he says that they know I am a good scrummager but I have to work on other aspects of my game. That is his bottom line. I know I can stand accused of moaning when under Cooke I have become England's most capped prop. But he has sought to replace me on a number of occasions and it would not take long to work out that he does not have 100 per cent faith in me. He has tried different players but none of them so far has come up to his expectations.

Cooke will be a hard act to follow because he is unique in England's development. The man who comes in for him eventually may have better managerial qualities in dealing with the Rugby Union but I do not think he will have the same professional attitude which Cooke has brought to the game. Cooke has headed up the England operation at the same time as rugby has taken definite steps away from its totally amateur ethos. I see no reason why he should not benefit. He is a proven motivator and I am sure people would want to know how his methods of motivation could be used in fields other than rugby or sport.

One of Cooke's decisions with which I take issue is to make Carling part of the England selection panel. I know that the England captain has always played some part in selection with a bit of advice on this player or that player. But my understanding is that Carling has a wider role than that and a vote if necessary. In my view it means that Carling is guaranteed a place which is neither good for him nor the team. It is all a matter of performance on the day if you are going to select the best team.

Because Cooke has come down so much on the side of the players I do not doubt that he has enemies within the Rugby Union who would have sought to replace him earlier if he had not been as successful as he has. Now there is no sense in anyone seeking to change him prior to the 1995 World Cup because so much preparation has to be locked into place and he can draw on the experience of reaching the 1991 final.

As far as I am concerned, I have never had a lengthy discussion with Cooke on how to play rugby and I don't suppose he would ever dream of telling me how to play at prop any more than I would dream of telling him how to manage a back line, even if I do have a few ideas. But I have no illusions. When Cooke considers I am no longer useful to him I will be out of the side. Usefulness does not always mean useful in terms of playing strength. Anyone who questions Cooke's captain is liable to be dropped for the simple reason that he believes the captain should have ultimate authority to such a degree that he allows the captain to run the final training session the day before an international match. Basically, I suppose, the captain is passing on the Geoff Cooke pattern to the players. Anyone who has watched England prepare in the last few years will recognise the Geoff Cooke pattern – meet on Wednesday evening, work out privately on Thursday and publicly on Friday when we run off about eight scrums and half a dozen line-outs. The captain who runs that relatively short Friday session is enhancing the image that he inspires his team.

When Cooke became manager in 1987 he studied England for one year and came to the conclusion that England needed a hero to become a substantial team. He then chose the youngest man in the side, the man he perhaps hoped would do everything he said because of his experience with him at other levels. The player he chose was then 22 years old, the youngest captain of England for 57 years, and was at the start of only his second international season. I am talking, of course, of William David Charles Carling OBE.

Chapter Fourteen

WILL CARLING – MY VIEW

Will Carling was a university student when I first became aware of him. He was on an Army scholarship to Durham while I was working in the family business and had my wife and three children to bring up. He was a back and I was a forward and there would have been little chance of our paths ever crossing but for rugby. I began to hear about him playing in the north and making an impact in the Divisional Championship which is where I first remember seeing him, a strong lad, well balanced, and a cut above anyone else of his age. The one factor which drew us together was that we first played for England in the same game, against France in Paris in 1988.

Will was just one of the boys like the rest of us trying to make a bit of progress. When he was made captain he was still the same young kid who had to call heads or tails before the match. Previous captains had loyalty to the other players but now, in the new era of England management, it seemed to me that Cooke had set up a situation where the captain's first loyalty was to him.

I do not know if Carling was aware of the backs–forwards divide in rugby at that early stage of his captaincy. Backs are usually the pretty boys who do not abuse themselves too much while forwards are different animals, older and able to enjoy the excesses of life. Forwards work as a unit which breeds loyalty, one to the other and all for one in defence of the unit, and are coached to be together. Carling's contact with forwards had been minimal and I am sure he had little idea of scrum or line-out play.

Carling could also have been intimidated by some of the long-standing backs. Rory Underwood had been around for a long time, since 1984, and Rob Andrew was much the same. Richard Hill had been in the squad for a few years. By comparison with these players Carling had done very little to earn the captaincy. But Carling had been reading psychology at Durham and I suppose that helps when you are dealing with such a mixed bunch of men as a rugby squad. When he bought himself out of the Army in the same year that he was made captain I decided he had a very professional way of looking at things.

Carling developed on three fronts: as a player, a captain, and a businessman. It was not long before he set up a company dealing in motivation packages and his position as England captain could not have harmed his business at all. Like everyone else who has been captain he had a limited lifespan in the job and knew that he would very quickly fade when someone else took over. Against that, Cooke had given him a long time as captain, at least a three-year period up to the end of the 1991 World Cup which no one had had before. Carling was not a selector in those early days but I am sure he had likes and dislikes on selection. It struck me that Cooke would want reasons why people should be in or out, not likes or dislikes.

What, for example, was the reason for dropping Paul Rendall? He had previously questioned Carling's decision-making capabilities and spelled out his views on the perennial question of who was to blame for wins and losses. Rendall said the backs should take responsibility for their mistakes, such as the one which cost the Welsh match at Cardiff in 1989. Carling maintained that the forwards should have been back to rescue that situation. When we were unsuccessful

Carling would blame the forwards for not controlling the game and presenting the ball quickly enough.

In the World Cup final, I believed we would continue the way we had throughout the tournament – from the opposition ten-metre line to their 22 the ball would be run in the right circumstances. From anywhere else on the pitch we would kick for position, either diagonally to the wing or box kicks and hit the catcher. Imagine my surprise when, from the first scrum on our ten-metre line, Carling ran and was tackled by Tim Horan and then Rory Underwood knocked on. Other forwards were surprised as well.

There have only been a few occasions when Carling has been called upon to make decisions about a style of play, and in my opinion his judgment has been less than perfect. I thought we needed to revert to the way we had been playing, but when Carling was asked at half-time by one of the forwards why we had changed pattern he said that if we kept playing the way we were we would score a lot of points in the second half. In my opinion, we lost the chance to win the World Cup on that basis. We had made it to the final playing one way and we had not practised sufficiently the running game which was now being called for. We should have stuck with what we knew to be successful.

When Carling was breaking through he was fortunate to play with a great distributing player like Kevin Simms alongside him. Simon Halliday, also solid, was with him for a while and then Jeremy Guscott came in as co-centre. That meant relating Carling to Guscott, inside centre to outside centre, and what Carling does or does not do. As soon as Geoff Cooke made Carling captain for a long period he became marketable.

How long should Carling be captain? There is no answer to that one because injury, unfortunately, can play such a part in decisions like that. People revered Bill Beaumont as captain and for leading the Grand Slam England team in 1980 but Beaumont came into the job because someone was injured and left it for the same reason. As I say, you cannot answer that one but it is true to say that a winning team does not necessarily have a good captain any more than a losing team has a bad captain. You could argue that England were on the up before Carling was captain and would have remained so.

Carling has turned, or been turned, into a very commercially orientated young man who knows his value. He has an agent to sell him and I am sure he is not being sold as a director of a management company but as England captain. There are plenty of guys in the City of London who are young and eligible and directors of companies but the difference is that they are not captain of England.

I am convinced Carling wanted me out in 1989 but I never had it out with him because he would deny it and because I want to continue to play for England. If I had had an argument where would it have got me, what would it have achieved? Yet, having wanted me out, I know that at the start of the 1993 Championship preparations he was asking around the pack who should be at tight-head prop and was told quite categorically that it was me.

I have sympathy for Carling because I know that away from the captaincy he is one of the lads, ready to compete on equal terms, have a drink, have fun. But given the captaincy and given the fact that that makes him commercially viable it is important that he keeps his profile and that he generates his own publicity. If he could earn £4,000 a day, for example, on a business pursuit and personal appearance, I would expect someone in my position to be able to command about £400. That is the market factor at work. I have no agent and do not sell myself on the commercial market but I have never been given a guarantee of being in the England side in the way that Carling has. When you are out, you are very quickly forgotten.

Carling is a loner, a man apart, not because he wants to be but because he has to be as captain. You can tell who your real friends are when you cannot influence whether players are chosen or not. Carling has never made clear to the players how much power he gradually acquired in the selection process. Maybe he should. He has little to worry about in his own position while Cooke is there but I think it is unlikely that he will look to play on once Cooke is no longer involved. Cooke, for the moment, has guaranteed Carling's future.

Nobody can tell what Carling would be like away from the captaincy. Prior to the commercialisation of the game, he was more a part of the team. We are all human and can see the advantages of being a star. You can see it in Brian Moore in the stern, hard image he portrays, in Gareth Chilcott and his shaven head which became his trademark, and with Jeremy Guscott and his individuality in a team framework. Carling needs none of these attributes because he is captain. Carling does not have Rory Underwood's try-scoring record or Guscott's ability or Peter Winterbottom's charisma but he has the captaincy and it will count for him.

To those who accuse me of sour grapes I reply that rugby is a 15-man game and no one does any more or any less than any other player on the pitch. Without all the guys around, what would Carling be? I begrudge him nothing and wish him luck. The Rugby Union should never have let the situation develop and instead of fudging the issue should have created a team deal and identity for commercial purposes so that the team and individuals would be marketed to exactly the same degree.

Carling has been boosted by being given the captaincy for a period of time, by being a good player, and because it would not be justified to drop him. In a side which lost more than it won – which is not the case in the Cooke–Carling era – both manager and captain would have been under threat. Cooke has stuck up for the players to the Rugby Union and has acted from a strong base. The Rugby Union can still reorganise the commercial side of the England squad by creating a level playing field to make everyone equal. All monies should be put into a trust and distributed on the basis of how long players are in the squad – the basis which is used by Player Vision.

Chapter Fifteen

THE MONEY GAME

The issue of money in the game and what the players can take out of what was once an amateur sport is never going to go away. I am aware that rugby was well into its second century by the time players began to do something in unison about benefiting from the game. But there is no stopping it now. I am quite sure that top players, the ones who draw full houses to international matches, will eventually be rewarded in proportion. The only question I cannot answer is when it will happen, but you can take it from me that none of today's players are going to be satisfied with no progress on the current financial position. Times are changing and for the various unions it is a matter of whether they lead and set patterns or whether the players or their agents or sponsors actually start setting a pace and leave the administrators to catch up.

Everyone in rugby enjoys talking about the merits of an amateur game but in reality amateurism went out of the window years ago. If every single player paid his club membership, paid his match fees, and funded himself to and from training you could say the framework of an amateur game still existed. But as any club administrator knows, that is no longer the case and has not been for years, long before I came into the game. There have always been perks around like tailor-made jobs, help with accommodation, and possibly a car. They still exist and player movement in many instances is a mixture of ambition and financial reality. The top half dozen clubs in England are going to attract ambitious players anyway but the minute those same clubs want to attract players to cover gaps in the team or plan for the future those players would not be human if they did not consider and did not ask what is in it for them.

You only have to be around a dressing-room or training session or in any club bar to catch up on the gossip of who is meant to be paying what or offering what in order to attract players. And thanks to the lengthy registration period demanded by the rules of the Courage Leagues in England, the recruiting has to be done months ahead of when the players need to be available. Some recruiting is going to be carried out on a cloak-and-dagger basis, persuasive phone calls, that sort of thing, but the ones who really influence players are other players. In the England squad you can see what other players are achieving at their clubs and soon discover what perks are on offer in the way of jobs, housing, cars, and travel expenses.

As for straight cash indictments, I can say only that I have heard all the rumours about this player and that player but I have no proof whatsoever that hundreds of pounds in ready cash is now changing hands for a select few each League Saturday. Nobody in England has ever offered me money to play or to win a match or lose one. I have never been offered money to join a club but there was a time when a South African province wanted me to go to South Africa for a full season, take my wife and family, on the understanding that all would be found. If I had been single I might have considered it. As it was I was never going to uproot my family for such an opportunity. I stayed at home.

I never really considered what players were getting or not getting when I first broke into senior club rugby. In those days you could play against Welsh clubs much more often than now and there was always talk about the gate money, or part of it, going into the players' boots. You could also be fairly certain that French players at a good many levels were being paid because it just seemed so obvious that the game there was structured that way and administrators from other countries simply looked the other way. Perhaps it was the language barrier.

Everything I have described so far has been part of rugby for as long as I can remember. What really altered the scene was the advent of the first World Cup in 1987, and the emergence of Italy as a country prepared to hire top players, usually from Australia or New Zealand and from several other countries as well, to play in their league where clubs have direct links with high-profile business corporations. The Italian scene is too obvious to be true and although David Campese might be considered a bit of joke by England players I am sure the Australian wing is deadly serious when he announces publicly that he is rugby's first millionaire. Who can argue? Campese has been a year-round rugby player for several years and in an amateur game you have to assume that someone is looking after him.

When I was with England in Australia in 1987 for the World Cup we soon began to hear the rumours of the very obvious commercialism going on across the water in New Zealand, the joint hosts of the competition. We never made it across the Tasman Sea for the late stages of the World Cup because of our quarter-final defeat against Wales but we heard what was going on. There was the high-profile TV advert involving Andy Dalton, then the New Zealand captain, who was seen driving a tractor and praising its virtues. Everyone in New Zealand would have known who Dalton was and players from Britain and Ireland were astonished to see Dalton in such a situation when they themselves could never had contemplated doing such a thing under the regulations of the time. The Scots were particularly amazed and incensed and I think the England squad would have been if they had seen the adverts at first hand. It might have stirred us into action a little earlier.

By the time the second World Cup was coming around in 1991 the England squad took a decision to investigate the commercial possibilities and set up an organisation which would benefit its members financially and legally under the rules of the day. You could then receive money for off-the-field activities providing they were not rugby related which meant that you could open a store (a favourite example, this, but I have not heard of any English player doing it) but not appear in an advert in your England shirt. We realised that we were regarded as pace-setters by players from the other home countries and at the same time that we might create suspicion in the minds of certain members of the Rugby Union committee who could see that the last vestiges of amateurism were being kicked out of the window. We had to make our scheme work and satisfy the Rugby Union because although the International Rugby Football Board, the game's overall ruling body, had approved the move towards this new commercialism they wanted each union to do its own policing.

England decided to form a company called Player Vision. The idea was that all monies which could be earned from off-the-field activities would be channelled into this and shared out among the squad members. It was clear to me that perhaps four players would have real commercial value, maybe one forward, a centre, a wing, and the goal kicker, but under this plan all would benefit. There was a bit of a grey area about how limiting the company would be on players extending their activities on an individual basis. Will Carling was concerned that we would be putting ourselves into conflict with the Rugby Union and there was always a possibility we could be dropped – which never materialised.

We wanted everything in place before the start of the 1991 Five Nations Championship and then to lead on to the World Cup. It would be fair to say at that stage that Carling was making the bullets and Brian Moore, a qualified solicitor, as well as the number one hooker, was firing the shots about what we should do. At the first joint meeting of the squad it was decided to link Player Vision with an organisation called WHJ Promotions run by the former England cricket captain Bob Willis and his brother David. Our information was that Bob Willis would be sympathetic to our needs and that he understood the way in which sporting bodies worked. None of the players had any experience of marketing agents and the only one in the squad with any marketing experience was Carling. We all had to go along with what was said to us and although the whole business was meant to be kept under wraps Willis announced that he was our agent which must have been a red rag to the bull for the Rugby Union.

The first game of the 1991 Championship was against Wales in Cardiff and my understanding was that Willis was negotiating for the players to be paid for post-match interviews. This meant that the players would not give free interviews afterwards because we would be cutting off a potential source of income. There was also a feeling left over from the 1990 game against Scotland that the press had gone in with sharpened pencils once we had lost up at Murrayfield. Some animosity lingered. Geoff Cooke wanted the 48-hour period before the game to be interview free for the players. We also believed that TV interviews were going to be paid for. In the light of that the players took a decision before the game that there would be no other interviews given afterwards. Cooke was not part of Player Vision but after we had beaten Wales he did not attend the usual press conference and neither did anyone else from the England squad. Things did get blown up a little after that, we took a lot of flak as a squad, and Cooke and Carling apologised for what had happened. Our corporate image took a bit of a blow as well and the end of the relationship with the Willis brothers was not far away.

Once Willis and Player Vision had parted company, Michael Coley, who was then the Rugby Union marketing executive at Twickenham, wanted to help with the next stage of developments and I set up a meeting with Coley and Moore which led to Coley entering into discussions with a number of companies regarding sponsorship of the squad. Coley was not informed when Player Vision signed an agreement with a company called Parallel Media almost on the eve of the World Cup. This was followed by the launch of the Run with the Ball campaign designed to give the England squad a high profile throughout the World Cup and raise funds at the same time. Some high figures of potential earnings were talked about. Estimates were as high as £10,000 for each player from the World Cup and the 1992 Five Nations Championship which followed. But at the end of that period each player received £1,000. Twenty-six players received that amount.

Run with the Ball had some good, straightforward aims. Because it was mixed in with the World Cup activities it capitalised on the high profile of the event and was targeted to attract youngsters to play. On top of that it would be generating money for the squad from agreements with sponsors. Seven companies signed up for the 1991–92 campaign and we looked set to achieve our aims. It came as a shock to me to discover in September 1992 that the operation was £16,000 in the red after the first year. We were told that income from the sponsors was insufficient to justify costs. We were told that the single record we made produced zero income after costs had been deducted. We were told that players' expenses for personal appearances had not been fully covered and that start-up costs had been higher than could be expected in any subsequent activity.

The first year of the Parallel Media operation was a shambles, partly due to intransigence on the part of the Rugby Union who chose to interpret the IRFB rulings in a negative way so that what was acceptable in other countries might not be acceptable in England. Players in Ireland, Scotland and Wales appeared to be striking better deals than in England. Parallel Media arranged certain functions in the first year which required player support and some players made no appearances at those functions. We were very unprofessional in our approach and needed to get our act together as much as Parallel Media. In the light of the first year's experiences I believe that has now been done. At the end of 1992, a new three-year contract was signed between Player Vision and Parallel Media. In February 1993 I received a further £1,083.38, tax paid, and there was a hope that each player would receive £3,000 for the 1992–93 season.

Obviously what we were doing as a group of players in trying to create a money-making campaign upset members of the Rugby Union who had complete support for the way the game had been run for years. When we decided to talk to some of those who we believed opposed us in 1991 I went to see Sandy Sanders, a man who had played prop for England and gone on to become treasurer and then president of the Rugby Union. He is a man of total integrity and told me he disagreed with players receiving money in any shape or form. He realised that times were changing but reminded me that in his day he bought his own kit. He felt that if the game had reached the stage where money was involved it might be time for him to step aside. I knew I would not change his position but I respected what he had to say. The

Rugby Union heard all the arguments and counter-arguments before voting our proposals through. The Rugby Union can still look at our annual accounts so they cannot complain that they do not know what is going on. Future generations of players might become much more assertive than we were . . . and more highly rewarded.

I think the Rugby Union is more flexible in all kinds of areas these days but not in the case of commercialism. The Rugby Union reflects its origins and to this day is rooted in public schools, universities, and the Services. For them playing is a matter of being able to afford it, whereas in other countries which do not have the same kind of history they are more commercially aware. England could always go back to more amateurism, not less, and other countries in the Northern Hemisphere might be tempted to follow them.

I do not envisage a professional game in our part of the world. I believe that only France and England could support a fully professional set-up because they could create corporate deals. There is no way that England would go along with France and disenfranchise Wales, Ireland and Scotland, which is why I think that the structure will stay roughly as it is.

Nothing much can change for me in the time I have left as a player but who can tell where the game will go when today's 20-year-olds start to make their influence felt with Player Vision and its like? The young player today has been introduced into a playing system in England with a widening League programme, continued Cup programme, Divisional Championship and international matches, at least five a season, tours most summers and a World Cup every four years. Most of this has been superimposed on the game in the last seven years and agreed to by people at the Rugby Union. What they have developed under their own noses is a sporting business which costs millions of pounds and raises millions of pounds and the whole continuation is based on a ready supply of players able to sustain themselves in this sort of competition year in, year out. Do you think England will ever play a 37-year-old again? Will anybody ever go on that long?

Players are going to look very seriously at their commitments through the season because there will be very little escape. England have switched over to 18 League matches per season in the national divisions and it will be interesting to see how many national squad players actually take part in all or most of those games. Until now the second half of each season has been the crowded, intense time with League, Cup, and international matches coming up week after week. Now the first half of the season has become full as well.

You could argue that the First Division in England could become professional but that would put it in isolation from the others, a break-away similar to the Rugby League last century, and that is not going to happen. There is talk of an Anglo–Welsh league but to set that up would depend on the two unions agreeing to come together to discuss it which seems unlikely at the moment. It would also become elitist, helping only a few. Maybe a knock-out eight-club event from the two countries is a better solution if that is what people want.

I have been playing top-of-the-League rugby with Wasps in front of crowds at Sudbury which do not go above 3,000 and are often much less. I take nothing from Wasps apart from occasional legitimate expenses. I believe in a fair world and if anyone gets a pound then all the other players should get a pound because we have the same commitment. You cannot blame players for wanting to take advantage of success, which is what we envisaged with Run with the Ball, but while the Rugby Union sticks to the rules which others interpret differently nothing can alter.

At senior club level you are given things rather than money. I have mentioned help with jobs, accommodation and cars but free kit and boots and maybe a training holiday also come into the list of possibilities. You could probably negotiate a one-off payment to change clubs but in England I think the best you can hope for in financial rewards is generous expenses. I still do not believe that anyone is receiving a weekly wage, despite all the conjecture. The big and successful clubs will continue to attract quality players without having to buy them in. In Wales, where there are fewer job opportunities, it is more important for clubs to be able to provide a subsidy to a player's living expenses. In Scotland and Ireland I have always thought that rugby was played by people who could afford to do so anyway.

I am not in Australia, South Africa, or New Zealand often enough to know exactly what happens there. But both the Australian and New Zealand Unions are pushing along fast with schemes to help their international players earn more and in South Africa professionalism is one of the by-products of isolation from the international game. How much longer the International Rugby Football Board will continue to oversee a game where double standards exist remains to be seen. The whole business of money in rugby should be thoroughly re-examined because on the one side is what the administrators publicly like to think is happening and on the other are all kinds of goldmines which are being exploited and opened up year by year. Why not admit openly that the situation exists world wide and draw up a new code of conduct on money to which all will adhere? The International Rugby Football Board, to which all the rugby countries belong, should take a lead and show that they mean business.

Will Carling is a perfect example of what can be achieved within the present regulations. He has set a pace for the professionalism which has produced a lot of benefits for other England players. He has set standards at the top which will filter down to other levels. Youngsters today can see what kind of figurehead he has become and when they see him driving around in his Mercedes they may feel they want to be like him. When the core of Carling's England team has broken up the door will have been well and truly opened and future players will benefit even more. Carling has moved the English game into a different world and has blazed a trail. He has created a precedent and the Rugby Union cannot walk away from that.

Chapter Sixteen

SOLE ALONE

For most of my senior playing time I have maintained my bodyweight of 15st 3lbs. My height is 5ft 10ins on size nine-and-a-half feet and I have an 18-inch neck, a 46-inch chest, and a 36-inch waist. I have never seriously pushed weights to see what that would do for me – I went once with my brother and found it boring – and although I have thought about pushing weights each summer I have not done it. When I was at school there was a gym in the car park and there was a time when I could not move 150lbs on the bar but by the time I was in the fourth year I could put it above my head.

Having the strength to play at prop is a matter of developing muscles over a period of time. Remember I was playing as a 17-year-old against men in club rugby and was developing continually by playing two or three times a week which was my normal commitment in those days. I simply went and found games and although I could have lifted weights all day long I do not believe it would have helped my muscle groups in the same way as so many scrums did. Now that there is a much more sophisticated approach to training and player development, people like Rex Hazledine, the Rugby Union's fitness adviser, still come up against the fact that there are so many variables in player requirements. People say rugby is heading for a situation where all players will be 6ft 2ins, weight 15st and be even timers but frankly I think that will never happen. The game continues to cater for all shapes and sizes which is one of its important characteristics.

I know that some of the younger props are into power lifting these days but I do not think that is an answer. It cannot make you a good scrummager and the only way to become one is to play as many games as you can, especially in the early part of the season. There are a lot of inherent dangers in front-row play and if it is done wrongly it can result in death from a broken neck. My suggestion flies in the face of so-called medical experts but I do not believe you should make scrums artificially high or de-power them. The lower the scrum goes, the better if it collapses because you fall on your face. The higher you pack, the more you can fall on the top of your head and get compression.

I do go to see teenagers who have been hurt and possibly paralysed in scrum accidents. It worries me that most PE teachers have not played in the front row and do not have an understanding of what happens in there with the various changes in pressure and angles. There are two boys I know who are in wheelchairs from injuries caused by playing rugby and have suffered as a result of poor technical coaching. If a scrum collapses and lads keep pushing, anything can happen.

The Rugby Union produce a pamphlet on front-row play which has my name on it and it shows a scrummaging style I disagree with. The best advice I can give if a scrum collapses is for everyone to stop pushing. At international level the pressure goes off immediately on a collapse because everyone is experienced enough to know the dangers. Older players usually allow a scrum to settle before the power goes on because they realise that there is so much dynamic work in a small area. I remember playing against Moseley once when I got my positioning slightly wrong, the hooker went to the ground as we engaged, and we curled over which gave me a stiff neck for a few days. Basically I try to have one foot forward when I scrummage which makes it difficult for a collapse to take place.

After all my years in the front row I do not feel that I look too bad. I can count the serious cuts and bumps on one hand: the scar on my forehead came from a head butt on me against Brixham, I needed some stitches in an ear playing against Ireland, and I have a few nicks around the eyes and some scars on the inside of my mouth. I have some cartilage damage on both legs but I have never had a day off work from injury. I have propped for England on many Saturday afternoons and gone to work on Monday morning, lifting furniture around with an aching back. My firm, you may gather, carries no passengers. I carry things around all day long, perhaps 70 or 80lb loads, and in that sense I am one of the few England players in recent times to be physically employed, Mike Teague and Jason Leonard being the others. I know that at the end of a day's work I do not feel like going to a running track to put in sprint work. But I go to train twice a week – it takes me two hours to drive there – reminding myself all the time that I do it as a hobby. You think rugby cannot take over your life but at the top it does and you are into a very professional commitment without the rewards, not financial rewards anyway. The rewards of playing, competing, and winning are something you measure for yourself.

From the moment you are chosen to play for England it takes over your life. In the week of a Twickenham game, for example, you train on the previous Sunday, work for two-and-a-half days, and from Wednesday evening until Sunday lunchtime are involved completely with the squad. Effectively your mind is on England for eight days running and the day is going to come when the players are in camp for a week to prepare for an international. I see that the All Blacks managed to assemble on a Tuesday evening to play the British Lions the following Saturday. Others will copy that.

It is no secret that I would have liked to have been with the Lions in New Zealand but I was not chosen. I heard the squad announced on Radio Five and was pleased for the four props who were picked: Jason Leonard, Nick Popplewell, Paul Burnell and Peter Wright. It was a while before I realised that I was not one of the standby props so my 1992–93 season was to end with a game for England Classicals against Spain in Madrid in May. On 1 June I began training for the new season in the knowledge that I had more targets to aim for with

Wasps, London and England. I had many letters of support and understanding when it was known that the Lions had not chosen me. I was grateful for all of them, especially one from Geoff Cooke who was managing the Lions. It did not alter my decision to play on, I would have done that even if I had gone with the Lions. I began 1993–94 as a current England player and what happens after that I have yet to discover. I just know that when I am no longer in the first team at Wasps I will continue to play on my own terms rather than let the game dictate to me which is the case at the moment.

Whatever level I eventually go out at I know that nothing will change for prop forwards – it is the first point of contact and the place where you start to win matches or lose them. Every scrum is different because so many factors change – who has the put in, where the scrum is, who is defending, who is attacking, what is the score, and how long is there left to play. All these different conditions affect a scrum. I usually play three or four scrums the same way and then deliberately change to keep my opponent guessing. Concentration is as vital as technique. You have to look, listen, and play the game at the same time, riding different pressures. Some clashes will have a higher profile than others – and the most publicised contests I had were against David Sole of Scotland.

Sole and I are definitely different people but our chosen sport brought us into conflict often enough over a period of five years or so, usually at the highest level. Then he quit, out of the game at 29 after being captain of Scotland and playing for the 1989 British Lions. If I had gone at the same age I would have remained unfulfilled in international rugby but David took the decision that there were other things in his life that need attention and rugby would have to go. It was a pity in one way because we had had some good contests and I would not have minded a few more.

People who have no idea will tell you that there was bad blood between Sole and I, and that after the things that happened between us on the pitch we had nothing to say to one another afterwards and never exchanged international shirts which is custom and practice in the game. The part about the shirts is true in that we did not exchange them after any of the England–Scotland games we shared. We did the exchange quietly and away from the intensity of an international day when we played in the same Barbarians side against the East Midlands at Northampton. That was our way of doing it and David, who was captain for the day, let me take a conversion which I enjoyed for its rarity value as much as anything else.

Sole had three-and-a-half years playing for Bath before he returned to Scotland and although he missed the 1986 Cup final at Twickenham between Bath and Wasps we came to grips the following year when the two clubs went to the final again. It was not an historic battle between us because Sole was hit on the head early on and was not at his best and says that he can remember very little of his only winning big-match day at Twickenham.

David had a lot to say about me in his life story *Heart and Sole* and to keep the balance of the argument I will repeat what he said about me:

Jeff is a strong, awkward customer and a useful enough tight-head prop but, in the sense that he habitually uses illegal means with which to put pressure on his opposite number, he is effectively cheating. Probyn likes to get off the loose-head's right shoulder and come down into the middle of the scrummage so that he can pressurise the opposition hooker.

He binds on the loose-head's left elbow and levers down on it. The laws state that props must bind on their opposite number by grasping the jersey of the upper shoulder or back. In my case this means that his right hand should rest on my left shoulder or back. Jeff, though, persists in employing the tactic of taking a fistful of jersey just at the left elbow and forcing down on it. This has a dual effect of destabilising his opposite number and of blocking the opposition's hooker's view down the tunnel so that his sight of the ball being delivered by the scrum-half is restricted. It is a dreadful indictment on international referees that Probyn is not pulled up short for it. It is blatantly illegal and everybody knows that he does it.

But if he can get away with it good luck to him. I'm not going to whinge. It's a tough old trade in the front row at international level and we all use whatever means are available to us to put one over on the opposition. However, if what is being done is illegal and the referee seems unable or unwilling to administer the law then the player who is on the receiving end of the illegal treatment just has to administer his own brand of justice even if it means taking the law into his own hands. That's what I did. Literally!

When Jeff grabs hold of the loose-head prop's left elbow, he simultaneously bores in on the opposition hooker. He strives to lock out with his right leg now in a position from which it can be quite easily reached by the opposition loose-head.

When Scotland came to Twickenham in 1991, Sole proved that my right leg could be easily reached by grabbing it and leaving me scrummaging on one leg. I said nothing to him during the game but afterwards in the hurly burly of the Rose Room at the ground, where players go for tea after the game, I mentioned to a journalist that what Sole had been doing was downright dangerous and unless it was stopped someone would break his neck.

I felt confident that I could handle whatever situation was created by Sole's moves on my leg because of my own strength and the fact that the England pack was playing well that day. But you can never tell what sort of pressures are going down with all kinds of problems. It was the wider effect on the game which worried me and I would not have wanted what Sole did to spread to other levels.

My comments and Sole's retaliatory remarks meant that the debate continued well into the following week with Sole saying that he would only use the tactic against me and that there was no deliberate attempt to injure anyone. He accused me of inventing my own scrummaging rules to suit the occasion. Certainly the Scots were trying plenty of things against me because John Jeffrey, their flanker, was attacking the grip I held on Sole's arm and it took a while for the referee to sort that out.

Sole was one of a handful of props who cut the left sleeve of his shirt off when playing against me. That said to me straightaway that he had a psychological block when I was against him. Many other props agreed with me that far from giving me no shirt to bind on Sole was actually admitting that I gave him a headache in the scrums. Even the Australians and New Zealanders became sucked into the chopped-sleeve debate. Steve McDowell of New Zealand turned up sleeveless in the opening game of the 1991 World Cup and so did Australia's

Tony Daly in the World Cup final. Even Bob Dwyer, the Australian coach, played into my hands by saying he thought I was a difficult customer and had given loose-head props problems over the years.

I look at the young props these days and see them coming into international rugby much earlier than I did and in that sense I know I am an exception. But the earlier players come in, the earlier they will leave. Whether you are capped at 21 or 31, the time you can spend in international rugby is about the same. So much depends on injuries. I have been fortunate in that nothing serious has happened to me but you can never tell. Cynics say I could have had problems if I bothered to push! But whether you are in a live scrum or up against a machine there is so much physical pressure on you and it is not something you can prepare for in five minutes. I believe the best props start coming into the game a long way back and you can see them at the age of 15 and 16 in schools sides and know they are going to progress.

Chapter Seventeen

MY ENGLAND MEN

You do not have to be a mathematical genius to work out that most of the forwards England choose are older than most of the backs. If this has meant that the England team has an us-and-them ring about it, it is hardly surprising. The forwards call the backs girls and the backs call the forwards donkeys. This is an amicable arrangement which has gone on for years, and even though managements like to bring the two groups together by making forwards and backs share rooms and things like that, I suppose there will continue to be a friendly rivalry between us.

Mostly the people in the England squad have been together a long time and know each other extremely well from sleeping, eating habits, lifestyle, big-match-day feelings and so on. Even though you are in your own private world when you prepare for an international you cannot help noticing how others try to cope with the situation. But it would be a lonely business if you did not have others around you, all with their different approaches and sense of humour. So here are my views on the majority of the men I have been playing alongside on England's behalf.

I will start at full-back with Simon Hodgkinson who in my book is the best we have had for years. He played a major part in the style we developed in 1990 and his 60 points in the 1991 Grand Slam campaign, a record in itself, shows how valuable he was to that achievement. A lot of people said he had frailties but I think he was safe under the high ball and put in crucial tackles when they were needed. He was also said to lack pace, and again I would disagree with that because he proved, with a hand in so many tries, that his positional sense and speed were good enough. His kicking was superb and he could put the ball over from all kinds of angles and distances in all kinds of conditions and under all sorts of pressures. He kept kicking us to victory in the last game of the 1991 Grand Slam against France and I think that was one of the best kicking performances that any player anywhere in the world has ever produced. He then ran into problems on the tour of Australia and Fiji and lost his place to Jon Webb and finally went out of the squad – which will allow him to perpetuate the myth that he never went near the bar while he was in the squad!

Webb was deceptive in that he was not as good as he seemed. He was not as good as Hodgy under the high ball and there were distance limitations on his goal kicking which came to the surface in one or two vital games such as the World Cup final and when we were trying to break that 10–8 Welsh lead in Cardiff in 1993. He was brought back into the side to provide pace from full-back which he did but I do not think he created any more tries than Hodgkinson did, though he scored more himself. He could also cost the team tries, 1993 against France being a case in point, but he took the opportunities England gave him once Bath became his club and sent him back towards the international stage.

Ian Hunter had a good start for England in that he scored a couple of tries on his debut against Canada and another against France at the start of the 1993 Championship and looked set fair for a long run in the side. I know he has been knocked around a bit by injuries since and it was a tragedy for him that he put his shoulder out in the first match of the British Lions tour of New Zealand and had to come home. I believe Ian has world-class potential, that he has an ability which is seldom seen which allows him to score tries when logic says there is nothing to be scored. When he is fit he is superbly fit and he has the physique and ability to become one of England's greatest-ever backs. I think he will continue for England where he began, as a wing, although he offers a powerful option at full-back. He is also a very forthright young man and if I were involved in management I would make sure that I sought his opinions and reacted to them, one way or another. He is also the only player I know to have been honest enough to admit that he was not 100 per cent fit for a game and pull out as he did against South Africa. Others would have gone on and taken a chance but he turned down his place, which is an absolute rarity.

The Underwood name has been on the England wing since 1984 through Rory and looks like staying there a lot longer now that his younger brother Tony is in the squad as well. Rory is a real enigma because on his day he is the complete world-class player but he has also been the cause of England losing more games than any other player. His concentration never seems to stay on the game longer than a ten-minute spell and I have to say that I think he cost us the Welsh games in 1989 and 1993 through dropping his concentration. I grant you that he has scored some great tries, mostly since 1988 when the team began to produce better football. He has turned games around with moments of sheer brilliance and some of his tries make the adjective exciting something of an understatement. He is a quiet teetotaller who does not get involved that much and I remember the difficult times he had sharing a room with Rendall in Portugal.

Rory complained that Rendall left a ring around the bath and did not make his bed. It probably came as a shock to Rory when Rendall brought some of the players in at 4.00 a.m. and said there was a party in the room and Rory was throwing it. Rory, of course, retired in 1992 and came back again the next season without much of a break, and without playing very much he returned to the England side which shows what the management think of him. It was hard on his brother Tony who had been playing consistently and was dropped to accommodate him. How many other players could have done that?

Tony Underwood works a lot harder than Rory on his game. Their pace is about the same but in commitment I think Tony is a league ahead. He has not yet got the same physical presence as Rory and that is an area he needs to work on. He carried an injury in Argentina in 1990 which belied his talent. He played most of the games almost on one leg out there and went backwards. But he has since improved so much, being prepared to learn all the time, and I expect him to have a long career and I will continue to encourage him to have the occasional glass of red wine.

Mark Bailey is another wing of my acquaintance. He had a couple of caps when I was young in 1984, sneaked in for another in the 1987 World Cup, one more in 1989, and then had two games in 1990 before England moved Simon Halliday, a centre, to his wing which I thought was a little strange. Bailey is one of the great characters of rugby and has this super intelligence which meant he could go to Cambridge University without doing a land economy degree as so many of their rugby players did at the time. I first saw him playing at Cambridge, tall and stocky, and he took a ball on our 22 and ran through the backs and half of the forwards to score under the posts. He was one of the best wings I ever played with, with top ability, understanding, and positional senses. When he was captain of London he made a series of after-match speeches with the then president of the Rugby Union, John Burgess, and after earning a rebuttal from Burgess one week Bailey followed up the next by saying: 'I would like to apologise to anyone I offended last week. It will not happen again. I have had a sense of humour bypass.'

Bailey is a Wasp. So is Chris Oti who started to make dents for England in my first year, 1988, and showed when he was fit that he is one of the most powerful wings we have ever had. He had a lot of confidence at his peak but injuries reduced that confidence and he does not take opponents on in the way he did in his younger days. He used to just go, now he stops and has a look. He is often out to lunch when he walks around with his Walkman plugged in, his ears smothered in sound. I remember in 1987 while preparing for an England B game that Chris was standing still when a move which ended with him passed by. 'Don't worry,' he said. 'I'll be there on the day.' Nigel Heslop, who had a short England career before going to rugby league, was a 100 per cent guy who was never destined to be one of the stars. I think they were looking to replace him from the moment they first chose him but in one of many solid performances he scored a cracker of a try against Scotland in 1991.

When Will Carling is a player and not captain he is much more relaxed. This comes through in his game because he has good hands, is fast and powerful, and tackles quite well and is not short on guts. He might have realised during the British Lions tour that life away from the captaincy has its rewards. I do not think he is a great decision-maker on the field but deserves his place on current form even if he is going to be challenged for it. Will has a caring personality away from whatever you think is his public stance. For example, when my son Jeffrey broke his back on a skiing trip to Italy and I went out there to bring him home Will was on the phone daily to my wife Jenny to see how things were and if there was anything he could do. He definitely has this pleasant side to his nature. I think he has been insecure in the England set-up because he was a young one in a team of experienced players and had to come to terms with that. He will take a practical joke and give one back – more so when he is not in his captain's mode.

Jeremy Guscott is our most talented player. He is fully aware of that and can allow himself a bit of conceit because he is so gifted. He has pace and vision and all the attributes you want at centre. I think Carling is jealous of his ability and does not give him the ball early enough and often enough. I think there are lots of examples of that. Many of Guscott's tries or breaks have come from miss moves where Will has not been involved with the ball. They had the potential to become a world-beating centre pairing but it has not happened on a sustained basis. I do not think Jerry has the ball enough and tends to hang on to it when he does. Look at how devastating Jerry is when he has played with Simon Halliday or Tim Horan or Scott Hastings. Jerry is his own man and does not get involved in team stuff too much. He does plenty on the commercial front as if to say that if Will can do it, so can I. He is a very professional model. He does not voice opinions much within the team because basically I do not think he gives a damn as long as he is in the team. He is calm and collected but capable of anger if he is blamed for a piece of bad play which he considers was not his fault. He would never do any harm to anyone because he is basically a nice bloke. I think it is fair to say I have never heard him argue about anything expect South Africa. Unless he sees changes in South Africa I cannot see him going there for the 1995 World Cup.

Since Rob Andrew plays for Wasps and London, as well as England, he is there at fly-half in most of the matches I play. He has long been known as Squeaky because of his clean-cut looks. He is a man who holds his own counsel and he has all the virtues which you would associate with a traditional England captain. Everything he does seems carefully planned and to a large degree he plays rugby that way as well. He is a great trainer and long after the Wasps club session is over at Sudbury he will be out there working on some aspect of the game. I regard him as a mechanical fly-half without a flow of natural ability. He is a manufactured player who works hard all the time on his game. He stands deep to give himself time and space to place his kicks. He does make breaks but because he is coming from a deep position they tend to be less effective. He had a strong partnership with Richard Hill whose speed and depth of pass gave Rob the time he wanted. He was unlucky to be dropped after Wales in 1993. Everyone was saying that Geoff Cooke is Rob's Dad when along comes the surprise that Rob is out of the team. It came as a surprise to me and probably a bigger surprise to Rob.

Two fly-halves who thought Cooke had a down on them are Peter Williams and Stuart Barnes. Williams was taken to the World Cup in 1987 and played three games but he could not command a place the next season and drifted away to rugby league. Barnes was capped way back in 1984 and has spent time since both in and out of the squad. I know down at Cardiff in 1993 he was on the bench for the 23rd time – and he was promoted for Andrew after Wales won. Barnes is very talented and has good vision. He kicks tactically as well as Rob and is a better goal kicker. He plays a very flat game and relies on a good scrum-half. He is very much his own man – he wants to run the backs and play the game his way. He will not toe the line for other people because he believes in one style of play and after all that time on the bench I am sure he would rather play than watch. The choice between Barnes and Andrew is not cut and dried. If Andrew had played against Ireland in 1993 we might have won because he would have been taking the ball deeper. Barnes was engulfed in that game. You could actually play them both in the same season, different men for different demands. I would not expect Andrew to stay out of the England team because Barnes plays his game so much on the edge.

Nigel Melville was scrum-half for England when I began and he was a most complete player who had a lot of bad luck with injuries. He was carried off against Ireland in 1988 at Twickenham, just after I started, and did not return. So I never knew what might be achieved with him, I was just sorry that we did not have a run together for a number of games. Richard Harding was Melville's understudy at the time, an experienced and erudite man who had a habit of taking his slippers and dressing-gown with him for use in the dressing-room. Richard distinguished himself on a tour of Australia when we visited a sheep farm and watched a lengthy exhibition of shearing. When the audience was asked if there were any questions. Richard posed this one to the farmer: 'What's your wife like in bed.' The audience collapsed, farmer embarrassed, and we went on our way. Richard went on his way as well. He captained England against Fiji in mid-summer 1988 – and never made the squad the following season. Maybe the fact that he was 36 had something to do with it.

Richard Hill has been around since 1984. He is one of the most combative players you could meet and for a while he seemed to hate everyone except players from his club, Bath. He is a great passer of the ball, has a good chip and some breaking ability, and his work with Rob Andrew in the first Grand Slam season was not appreciated as much as it should have been. In the World Cup final he was playing to instructions to ship the ball out all the time so he offered no threat close to the scrum and allowed Australia to fan out and cover all of our back moves. He is a 100 per cent honest man, involved in the committee of Player Vision in its formative times, and the one guy who would stand up and be counted when things did not go as they should have. During the World Cup Hill argued with Carling when Will questioned the way tactics were decided on the field. Will castigated the other backs but Hill told him that he was captain and if he was not happy with the way things were being done he was the next man outside Rob Andrew and should see himself what was meant to happen. It is probably one of the reasons why Hill was later dropped.

Dewi Morris was scrum-half in 1989 and again in 1992 and 1993 and for what he has achieved in a short time he is almost a miracle man, coming from the Winnington Park Club to a cap. His weakness is his pass and he knows that and works continually to improve. Passing is not a natural thing to him and under pressure it will break down so his first option is to break and he is a great runner, tremendous at finding gaps. With Dean Richards alongside him he can run all day because Dean will create the space for him and take the ball from him at the right moment. If Dewi can improve his passing permanently he will be in the side for a while. He is a good man on the road, full of practical jokes and with a distinctive laugh.

Dean Richards is one of the greatest players to pull on the England number eight shirt. Ultimately he has the respect of every forward he has played with or against. He is dedicated to the team and treats the squad as a family, feeling we should share all the ups and downs together. He will always say what he feels and if he thinks he has upset someone he will not let sleeping dogs lie and will want to sort it out. As a player we all know there are limitations to his pace and that he is not the greatest off the ball. But he is so often in the right place at the right time and the whole back row effort gels when he is there, he just has this immense physical presence. You could see Scotland sag for instance in 1992 when Tim Rodber went off injured and Richards came off the bench to play. It was a lift to us, a real downer to them. Dean's problem is whether he can regain a place now that Ben Clarke has come in at number eight. Maybe if England slip they will want Dean back to anchor them. I do not see him going into the second row, it will be number eight or nothing.

Ben Clarke could not stop scoring pushover tries when he first broke into the London team and he keeps making so much progress year by year that you have to think of him as a long-standing choice for England. He has to learn that the game is not always played on attack, where he is outstanding, and I can see plenty of reasons why England should cap the 1993 British Lions and play Clarke at number six and Richards at number eight for a couple of years or so. There will be a lot of competition for England back-row places with so many youngsters around and Clarke has a big head start. He is good with the ball in his hands, hard to stop, but needs to be careful not to get isolated. He cannot turn a match with defence like Richards can, but he can learn.

Peter Winterbottom is by far the best flanker England have had but Gary Rees would come close to him. Winterbottom is a loner and looks at what is in anything for him. He has played rugby like a professional, moving clubs, moving countries, when it has suited him. Rugby gave him the chance to travel and to see and experience other lifestyles. He has called the back-row moves for England and leads the pack but he did not have the ambition to be England captain like Will Carling or Brian Moore. Winters is often called the hardest England player of modern times but we all cut and we all bleed. Anyone who plays international rugby has to be hard because you get hit and you have to carry on. Winters had a very strong mental attitude which in many ways would be beyond most players, especially those who are trying to succeed him. Winters has been a major player on the fun side as well, a cutting edge to John Olver's wit. They have pulled tours around with their humour.

Mike Teague was the subject of a terrible misjudgement by me in 1988 when I first really came across him. I thought he had been around for a while and was happy to leave his England career at a few caps and drift away. I made the mistake of saying this to him and he very firmly rebuffed my remark and told me he was definitely going to have another go. Of course he did it. He has played for England at number eight and blindside flanker without ever being a specialist in either place which shows what a good adaptable forward he became. England have used him a lot as a battering ram which works against certain opposition who do not have the physical resources to stand up to it. In the World Cup Teague was at number eight for his running while Mick Skinner played at blind side for his tackling. I go back longer with Skinner than Teague because we used to be on opposite sides when I was at Richmond and Skinner was at Blackheath. But Teague is one of those solid Gloucester boys, 100 per cent committed to England, who has had lots of big moments. Teague has been the butt of many jokes from Winterbottom and I expect he will get his own back in the end.

The Skinner I first met is not as big and solid as today's version, the man always looking for the big tackle. He is larger than life, which is no illusion, and that is also his serious side. I have never known him punch anyone but his tackle is immense, he can make a whole stadium wince with one of his big hits. Even tacklers like that have their limitations but pace is not one of them as he has proved so often by being the first man to race up and congratulate an England try scorer, take the ball, and trot off happily down the pitch with the cameras on him.

Skinner sets out to enjoy himself. In 1987 when he was flown out with the World Cup squad in Australia there was some trepidation among the selectors about his lifestyle. He was allocated to me because it was thought I would keep him on the straight and narrow. I do have a bond with him because I think he is a genuine nice guy who can also do things which grate. But he is a brutally honest guy and some people do not like that. I guess Skinner knew at one session that he would never be picked again. Like me he thought that Dick Best as coach did not want him back in the side after 1992. He asked them to leave a tackle bag on the training pitch in remembrance of him. The people who suffered Skinner's big hits would smile at that.

I have been in a lot of squads and teams with Gary Rees who first turned up in 1984 vowing to take Winterbottom's place. He never quite managed that on a regular basis but he piled up caps, many of them as a replacement, and shared with Winterbottom the reputation of being a flanker people hated to play against. Rees had a professional wrap-up tackle which put the opposing player on the ground and allowed the ball out on Rees's side. It worked all over the place but Rees had to pay a penalty because his back would be to the opposition and he was well raked by many teams. Not that he seemed to mind these maps of the motorway system being left on his back. You could never kick him off the ball. He had a great ankle-tap tackle and a wonderful shirt-pull technique and chattered on endlessly to referees with all kinds of helpful suggestions. When we played Fiji in Suva in 1988 Rees asked the referee if one of the Fijian forwards could do what he was doing at the base of the ruck. The referee agreed that it was wrong, awarded a penalty, and the Fijian rose to deliver a big blow on to Rees's mouth which left him with a painful split and an uncomfortable journey back to London. But England won, the Fijian was sent off, and Rees recovered. He would have enjoyed all that.

Paul Ackford and I go back to the seventies when we both played for Surrey. He was a number five jumper in those days and he was a wimp as well. He was a rising star beyond doubt but if he got an elbow he was out of the game, it was that easy. He was out of the scene for a long while as a result but when he played for London against Australia in 1988 he played as if it was his last game at that level, was very relaxed, and just took off. He would no longer stand for intimidation and became a key player overnight, fulfilling the promise of years before. He went to the front of the line-out and found there was some space for him to play in, all based on his timing and the lifts that the support players could give him. Ackford and Wade Dooley both gave terrific stick off the field and were a real human combination. Ackford retired after the World Cup and I think that was a year too early. But if he had gone on, Dooley would have been dropped for Martin Bayfield to be brought in to develop as a number five jumper. Ackford was never afraid to voice his opinion, argue his case, but he was a diplomat as well.

Dooley has packed behind me in hundreds upon hundreds of scrums. You ask, he provides. He is A grade immense, no argument. He is a quiet guy, never one to rock the boat, enjoys his rugby and knows how to enjoy himself when it is over. He has relaxed over the last couple of years as he has come to the top of the game. He is not a fighting man but looks after himself when he has to and he looks after his friends as well. He has been a cornerstone of the England side and you cannot always measure his contribution adequately.

The best thing to say is have a look at England when he has gone and you will see an England side that lacks a core. He will be a hard man to replace, a big physical man with total pride in his fitness and level of performance. He makes space for other players to play and the way he does that is his own, a combination of all the years of experience coupled with his size and ability. He certainly made a difference to my play because you do not need to work so hard to help him and that lets you contribute more in other ways.

173

Bayfield has been in the second row for a couple of years and had to learn quickly when he was pitched in against Fiji and Australia in 1991. Given space he is a very effective jumper but does not yet have a physical presence. He will learn to become more of a physical animal but needs two or three years. He could be dropped within that period and still come back as a player of real quality. He is still a rarity in English rugby at 6ft 10ins and people have to remember that because we have not developed one like him before he is going to need some nurturing along the way.

Brian Moore has been alongside me in all but two of my England matches, against the Barbarians and Argentina. He became England's most capped hooker in 1993 and in many ways is the ultimate competitor because he plays to win whatever he does. He is dedicated to rugby and will sacrifice almost anything to play for England. Moore works hard at his game and although he is not the best hooker by a long chalk, he is a better rugby player than John Olver, his deputy, even if Olver is the better technical hooker. Moore has more all-round ability and more of a physical presence.

Moore is very intelligent and realises the commercial value of being seen as the abrasive competitor. Whoever is pack leader, Moore does it anyway and talks a lot of good sense in a quiet, communicative way when there is a stoppage of play and time to pass thoughts on. I think he does a lot of other shouting up and down the pitch for the benefit of microphones and cameras. He is a good analyst and looks beyond the first phase of play. We were trying to develop a move once which was deliberately planned to go wrong so that we could create a little more space. Moore said from the start it would not work. It never did, and we abandoned it.

Moore is witty, one of four or five comic guys in the squad, and has one of the worst laughs. He is very serious to play with and will have a go at me for doing what I want in a scrum rather than what he wants. He might call an eight-man shove but if I don't feel it, if it's not right, I don't do it and that annoys him. We understand perfectly what we are trying to do and I have a lot of time for him. But if he is true to himself he would admit there are things he would not have done other than to keep his place.

How can I say if I am a friend of his or anyone else? We meet only around rugby things and not much else. But we would have dinner together, his place or mine. There are no greys in Brian Moore's life, just stark black, stark white. We have shared some secrets which are still secrets and will remain secrets. I know that when he leaves the game he will become an even higher flier in the City but he has rugby in his sights for a while – 1994 will be a key year for him. Once he stops you might not see Moore around rugby for a while. But he will be back, never fear.

Olver had been the bench hooker 32 times by 1993 and has three caps. Something drives him on and I have to say that his contribution to the England team effort is immeasurable. He still feels pain at not being picked and I cannot imagine what it is like to sit at team announcements time after time and not hear your name called too often. He should have had a couple more caps but he has taken all that over the years and come back for more. He has led from the front of the field and keeps the boredom out of the squad with some new prank or joke.

I would still choose Moore over Olver if it was left to me for the reasons I have given. Olver has been the father confessor to most people in the team because when you are hacked off with something you can talk it through with him and feel you are getting somewhere. After all, if you are in the team he is worse off than you. After a game Olver is always the first to shake hands with Moore and he really means it. He wants that place and I know he would give what teeth he has left for it and he would not let England down.

Paul Rendall played for England from 1984 to 1991 and was the best line-out forward in the world because every lock dreamed of playing with him. He had the ability to turn an average line-out jumper into a star. All you had to do was select which floor of the line-out hotel you wanted to reach and Paul would take you there. So simple, and true. He was good at lifting his man on our throw and he would be creating space and mayhem on theirs. He was instrumental in my joining Wasps from Richmond. After a game between the two clubs, Alan Black, the Wasps coach, asked what was going wrong in the front row and Paul said you had better ask Probyn. Paul saw me through many experiences and persuaded me to put in the extra training which was necessary if I was going to win caps.

We developed a good relationship on and off the field and I had to bow to him because he was an established character when I arrived. He has a great fund of stories, some of them so long they would make *War and Peace* seem like a pamphlet but he talked a lot of sense when he had to. He was there when I played my first game for England in Paris and all I could think about was whether I was going to be good enough. 'Don't worry, stay calm,' said Rendall's voice in my ear as we waited to go out. 'Just get on with your game, forget the stadium, forget the 50,000 crowd, just think of the ten million watching at home on television!'

He told me never to dwell on a mistake, just keep concentrating on the next piece of play. He encouraged my style of play, offered bits of advice and criticism here and there, and I developed my own technique at the front of the line-out from listening to him and watching what he did in the middle of the line-out. If I am the most destructive prop around, then Paul was the most constructive at loose-head. Against him there was never an easy scrum and no matter what you did to him you could never get near to his hooker. That is why he was outstanding.

Rendall is known throughout the game as The Judge, because he was the best judge, handing out harsh punishments which people had to suffer. He ordered several players at the Players' Court to shave off their moustaches in Australia and made Brian Moore drink out of a dog bowl and wear a collar. John Bentley, a three-quarter from Sale, was tied to a tree in Mackay, Queensland, and made to sing *Chanson D'Amour* every ten minutes for three hours. Perhaps that is why Bentley turned rugby league. But The Judge did it all with a touch of style and is much respected. He was one of those men who could drink all night long, sleep for an hour, and then train for four hours in 90 degrees. I know that playing for England cost him, as a self-employed man, a lot of money but I hope he had as much pleasure and satisfaction as the rest of us did from knowing and playing with him.

Jason Leonard followed Paul into the England loose-head slot. I first met him in Bucharest when he was on the bench for the England under-21 team, we played in the same B team against Fiji, and I was there when he was first capped in Argentina in 1990. He was obviously very strong and fit but technically had a lot of work to do. He enjoys a laugh and a drink and trains like hell, following fitness routines to the letter. His first two caps were against Argentina's Diego Cash who gave him a bit of a roasting the first time out but Jason caught up fast and did not struggle the following week against the same opponent. I am sure England decided then to go with Jason until someone destroyed him but he never was. He has struggled a couple of times against Paul Burnell of Scotland and also against Richard Loe when he played New Zealand in the World Cup. But if he stays fit he will become the most capped prop in England.

The player I had in my sights all the time was Gary Pearce of Northampton who had 36 caps, then a record, by the time I won the place over him in 1988. I respect him enough to say that if he was picked now I would accept it even if I did not like it. We have had a love-hate relationship over the years because we both believe we are one and two in the country but just disagree about the order. He was among the first to send congratulations when I was chosen in 1988 and again when I broke his record and won my 37th cap. He is a great chap, very quiet and thoughtful until he decides to celebrate. At the end of the Australia tour in 1991 Pearce decided that it was time to celebrate and during a session in a bar near to our hotel in the Sydney suburb of Manly, in walked one of the rugby writers who Pearce decided should buy a round of drinks. Pearce upended the writer and held him gently by the throat until he agreed to stand his corner. Later I decided to take Gary to his room but he burst out of the lift on a lower floor, heading for the management table in the restaurant. I had to put in one of my best tackles to cut him off. I had to sit on him for a while to keep him still and then put him into my room so that I could keep an eye on him. As I say, he is very quiet and thoughtful.

Gareth Chilcott is another England prop I have shared a few scrums with, for and against. He can play both sides of the front row but his fame has come more from being a larger than life character who has come through various sendings-off and bans without serious damage. People called him a fat boy which belied the fact that he was a good ball handler and could make a vital contribution to a game in that way. He is a good, solid prop, not world class but you know he is there. I think we punched each other once in all of our games which shows there is some mutual respect.

This chapter would not be complete without allowing someone the chance to take a look at me – so, with a little trepidation, I hand over to Paul Rendall:

The first time I remember seeing Jeffrey was when he was at Richmond. I had one or two games against him and at that time he was understudy to a prop named Willie Dickenson who had set the same sort of style and was out of the same stable. But Willie was straight down as a prop whereas Jeff screws through a bit.

At Wasps, I would be up against Jeff a lot in training and we did a lot of one-on-one work and showed each other a few tricks. I was often against him in England sessions as well and although a lot of them would end in stalemate it usually depended on who had the weight behind them.

Around the field he has this uncanny ability to pop up everywhere and he is very good at rucking and mauling and ferreting the ball out. You have to remember that in the front row, your opponents usually speak for you and for years at Wasps we had a good front row with not much else behind which made Jeff work that bit harder. He became one of the top props in the world, up there with players like Jean Pierre Garuet and Robert Paperemborde of France. The way Jeff scrummages is the way France had been scrummaging for some ten years and there was no point in shouting that they were illegal because they were killing us at the time. France would drive on the opposing hooker, creating compression because they had three on two players rather than three against three. We modelled ourselves on the French style at Wasps, driving on to the loose-head prop and hooker and it was very productive.

Jeff does a lot of hard work in his job which keeps him in shape and there is no doubt that he is tough, very tough. He has taken a lot of clouts which would probably have held a few other people down, wondering if they should carry on. When Jeff had his first cap in France he took an almighty belt in the first line-out from Pascal Ondarts as a welcome to Paris and just shook his head and got on with it. I don't think there is a prop anywhere who would say Jeff is easy. He has earned a lot of respect and I doubt if there is anyone in the front-row world, including those who were chosen at prop, who does not believe he should have gone to New Zealand with the 1993 British Lions.

I have shared rooms with Jeff in many hotels and it has always been a nightmare. He is the worst roomie ever. There are not many people who will share with him which became obvious to me on the 1987 World Cup trip when he was in with me for three weeks. When he finally went in with someone else, Micky Skinner I believe, they gave me a suite to rest. His snoring is the chief problem because it goes up to a high note which wakes him up, and everyone else, and then he starts again. He also has a special relationship with television. If he walks into a room the set has to be switched on. You can go to sleep and the set will be on and wake up with it still on and Jeff will be watching no matter what it is. He will argue with the television, even with a cookery programme, if the mood takes him. When he is not doing that he might be making his telephone noise which is so perfect that people pick up phones which they think are ringing or his owl noise which is equally convincing.